3 Days to a Raise

A Woman's secret to making a lot more money

Bethany A. Williams

Dedication

I have a mission, and that mission is to transform the world for working executives everywhere. My journey has taken me near and far and everywhere in between. In pursuit of my passion, many have supported me to make it all possible. I want to give thanks to many of those that make up my support system:

To my loving and adoring children; Heather, Brandon & Caleb, thank you for your continued love and ever present support.

In the process of writing this book, I went through a divorce and am thankful for the people that stood by me, held my hand, hugged me when I needed it, and were there with a listening ear; my editor Amy VanVleck; Jestin Jose; my publicists in NY that keep me moving in the right direction, Hank and Steve; the amazing writer and coach that kept me in line, Terri Trespicio; my media trainer, Jani Moon; my best friend Laura Harrison; and my loving parents James and Elois Eastman. It would be impossible to list everyone, so many apologies for anyone I've missed. Without all of you, none of this would be possible.

A final thank you to my fans that continue to buy my books, buy my products, attend my speeches, and help me to live my dreams.

I love you all,

Bethany Williams

Contents

DAY 1: PERSPECTIVE: *Identifying Your Correct Pay & Closing the Wage Gap* _____ **8**

DAY 2: RESEARCH & LEARN: *The 11 New Rules for Getting Paid* _____ **25**

Rule#1: STOP Protecting Others More than Yourself 25

Rule #2: Women; Assume you're (at least) 30% underpaid ..30

Rule #3: Don't Confuse Self Doubt with Reality 36

Rule #4: Sitting Back in Silence Won't Get You Ahead........46

Rule #5:Taking Less Money Makes You Worth Less 49

Rule #6: Be the CEO of Your Career.................................52

Rule #7: Don't Let Past Disappointments STOP You from Moving Ahead 62

Rule #8: Know Your Value & Worth 64

Rule #9: There is More to Compensation than Cash..............70

Rule #10: Don't Be Afraid to Talk Numbers With Your Network 81

Rule #11: See 'No' As a Speed Bump, Not a Stop Light......84

DAY 3: Prepare Your Exit Plan & Go Ask for a Raise _ 86
Start with an exit plan
You have to ask
Understanding your boss
Appendix: Not-for-Profit Company Research Guide   94

Appendix: For-Profit Company Research Guide 97

1

Bethany A. Williams

3 Days to a Raise

Prologue

You are about to embark on an important personal journey to more job satisfaction and higher pay. The new rules for getting paid in this book will give you with the information necessary to fight the corporate Goliath and win. I've sat at the leadership table, surrounded by all men, and I've wondered. How did I get here? Amidst a market where women only land in senior leadership positions 8% of the time, and women only account for high wage earners 2% of the time, how did I end up at this table, right here, right now? I fought for it. **I outline the 11 rules for getting paid in this book, and many of them apply to both men and women.** I've specifically included tips that propel women forward. I'll tell you exactly what is holding you back and how to change it. I'll teach you how to do all the things you are not doing; overcoming your faulty belief systems, negotiating, and asking. I've identified how true wealth is gained in options and stock grants, and I've funneled immense resources and energy into focusing YOU on how to uniquely describe your skill sets and capabilities to get you the pay and the positions that you deserve. I believe you can change your circumstances, increase your pay, and help equalize the pay gap. You can change your circumstances as fast as you can read this book!

It hasn't always been easy. I often think back to my itty-bitty apartment in Pacific Beach, California. There were many months that I wasn't sure I'd be able to pay the rent, fearing that I'd be thrown out into homelessness with my then 2-year-old daughter. I was scared. I was alone. My husband had left me to raise her alone. I had no one to turn to. And my salary, even though I had a substantial management position at a hospital, certainly wasn't enough to pay the bills for both of us. After paying the bills, I had only $35 a week to buy groceries for us. We ate a lot of pasta. I told her that we were vegetarians because I simply couldn't afford to buy meat and didn't want her thinking that we were poor. She never seemed to notice what we didn't have, but seemed to revel in our close relationship. Her emotional needs were met. I fought hard to make a better life. I decided it had to be different. I desperately wanted it to change.

Although I struggled, I knew that I was smart. I had graduated second in my class, with a 3.989 GPA, and had been promoted frequently. The pay increases where I worked were capped at 5% per promotion and because I'd hired in at a very low rate, even after four promotions, I was still severely under-compensated. I fought for raises. Each one felt like life or death, food or no food, a place to live or potentially being homeless.

I found that persistence did indeed pay off. I achieved higher starting salaries and pay raises. I negotiated for better packages. I earned a better living that provided a better lifestyle for my family despite working in a job market that wasn't supportive of higher pay and promotions for women.

With increased salaries and higher positions, it afforded me money to pay for domestic help. I hired nannies and housekeepers. I outsourced components of my life that I didn't want to do or didn't have time to do. I hired pool cleaners, lawn maintenance staff, cooks, stylists, personal shoppers, drivers, and more. I put money into children's college funds, traveled around the world, and live a charmed life. I went from being a broke, single parent who

3 Days to a Raise

used to dye her own hair- with oftentimes poor results, to being able to afford the best hair stylists. I stood up for myself. I used the new rules for getting paid and they worked brilliantly. I have propelled myself to one of the highest paid women in my industry. You can benefit from these same rules. You can effect change in your salary and transform your life. **You can move in whatever direction that you want to move.** The strategy and simple formulas are all right here in the pages of this book.

You can make this dramatic shift, in as little as 3 days, or less. I've outlined the book to follow this 3 days outline:

Day 1 PERSPECTIVE
Closing the Wage Gap

Spend time learning the secrets and get a good handle on perspective. Without perspective and knowledge, the ball will stop short of the goal. You need this basic foundation for the remainder of the journey. What are you worth?

Day 2 RESEARCH & LEARN
The new rules for getting paid

Once you understand the secrets and pay practice norms, it will be time for you to figure out your market value, document your successes and begin applying the knowledge to YOU. Make it personal.

This is an important often missed step on the journey. Make a plan for you. Become the CEO of your career and your earnings. Begin practicing your ask.

Day 3 GO ASK
Prepare your exit plan and go ask for the raise

Now that you've done your homework, it will be time to move forward with action. Know what you are asking for, prepare for the ask, and make an exit plan to give you great options and put yourself into a position to be ready to negotiate your raise. This last step will help you score that raise. I'm here with you on the journey.

3 Days to a Raise

DAY 1: PERSPECTIVE:
Identifying Your Correct Pay &
Closing the Wage Gap

What you don't know is hurting you

Do you ever feel like you're not making what you should be making and you deserve to make what you are worth? If you feel that way, there is a probability that you are being underpaid in your current position and living in oblivion. The higher you climb, there is an unfortunate reluctance by your boss and company to adequately match your salary to market benchmarks. In the situations where it exists, the pay differences are blinding. It shows up most often when you have worked for the same company for several years, or if you've been promoted several times and taken on additional responsibilities and work. For non-negotiators and women and men who don't ask, it is probable that even if you haven't received numerous promotions or been at a company for numerous years, your wage may not be keeping up with the cost of living increases and other market variables. **You are stuck making much less than you should be making with no plan and no way out.**

Without research and an eye on the market, you have ended up working in a job that should pay you considerably more than you are making. What you don't know is definitely hurting you and there are three branches out of this pit: knowledge, transparency, and action.

Company pay policies that keep pay a secret make it harder to identify. Companies may threaten to fire employees that share salary data. You don't know that you are being short changed, Per nation.com, " The big winner in this game of secrecy is the boss, who profits directly from the ignorance and pliability of workers who don't grasp their own economic situation. "[1]You are being underpaid. Statistics say that women earn 20-30% less than their male counterparts, but in reality, that percentage is much higher. Truthfully, sometimes it is easier not to know. Even men suffer from making less. Often they don't ask, they take what is offered and you settle into a 'it is as good as it can be' mindset.

When it comes to pay practices for women, we are living behind the times. The Equal Pay Act was signed into law by John F Kennedy on June 10, 1963. That was over 50 years ago, yet we still are not moving the needle towards accomplishing equal pay. Many are hanging out in their positions, stranded, not upwardly mobile, without exercising freedom or gaining political power to mandate change. The statistics do not reflect what is happening in the pay world for a variety of roles, but, especially not for professional women. In many roles, it is far worse than the statistics reflect. You could be receiving considerably less pay than you should be making. You may be underpaid by 60%, 70%, or even 100% and not even know it, if the hundreds of women I've met and helped increase their pay are any indication of what could be happening to you.

Women are struggling to make it into leadership positions and lagging behind in top earner categories. Women comprise 50.8% of the U.S. population, earning almost 60% of both undergraduate and graduate degrees. Women also hold nearly 52% of all professional-level jobs, yet American women lag substantially behind men when it

3 Days to a Raise

comes to their representation in leadership positions.[2]
Women are only represented in 2.5% of the top earners in
companies. So even when you make it to the top, which is
rare, you aren't being paid adequately most every time for
the actual work that you do. The men are in the top earner
categories 97.5% of the time and making it into high-level
leadership positions 92%. of the time That speaks
volumes. This is not right or fair, and we can no longer just
ignore the obvious statistics. Woman or man, YOU control
your earnings and can change these facts. You can make a
difference in your pay and your life immediately.

It starts with YOU

You can change this right now. It starts with awareness,
and reading this book is going to give you with knowledge.
You will have what you need to take action. You cannot
afford to be left out on knowledge on the subject of your
pay and the laws that protect it. It is time for change. It is
time for action.

It is time to stop being the victims of a system that is not
built to improve itself and begin taking control of your
wages and income. To solve this, you need to become an
expert at understanding your power, learning about your
worth, acknowledging your weakness to ask, and learning
valuable negotiation skills for the salaries and pay that you
deserve. You are doing the work: why not collect the pay?

Several years ago, I began to coach executives towards
success. What I've discovered along this journey will shock
you, it will confound you, it will anger you. I set out to
help executives find their career footing as they yearned to
climb the corporate ladder. What I discovered was a nasty,

very well-kept secret: women are being drastically underpaid. I'm referring to compensation that is 70-80% or even sometimes 100%-300% below your male counterparts. Soon I discovered that were men as well that fell in this category. Without the knowledge that it was happening, they had slipped well below what they should be making.

How is this happening?

How is this even possible in a market where the fact that women make less is consistently denied? How do employers pay women less? They simply keep you in the wrong job code, pay you the wrong salary or expand your responsibilities over the years without performing a timely market analysis on the position. Sometimes they simply don't pay you for a new role you've accepted or possibly, you just haven't negotiated for the pay that you should be making. Your pay shortfall could be due to the fact that you are not demanding more. Since you are loyal to a fault, you don't speak up. You remain silent, excited that you have a job when many don't. I'm guilty. You've probably had it happen to you and you may not even know it.

It is an appalling national epidemic that no one wants to discuss, publicize, admit, nor do they know how to resolve this issue. The same men that would need to fix it have limited budgets: if they correct your salary; they and others will make less. Without more women at the top pushing for change and creating the solution, the epidemic continues to spread and is not resolved. Hence our ability to continue this trend 50 years after the passing of the Equal Pay Act.

3 Days to a Raise

The male leaders keep this secret, and we sit by and let it continue, unaware of our power, our voice, and our ability to stand up for change and make it happen. The gap has become so wide, that in some cases, the fix poses a considerable burden to companies. As the gap widens, so does the solution.

I've seen it. I've witnessed it firsthand. I too have fallen victim to such pay discrepancies. I was in the wrong job code for almost three years inside a Fortune 500 company. I had more than 30 emails from the company that said they would correct it. They did not correct it while I worked there. It took quitting, and a letter post leaving in order to get compensated for the salary that I negotiated when I accepted the job. The three men hired at the same time, into the same role, were put in the correct job classification and paid their negotiated amount. This is ludicrous. These are not small companies doing this, these are Fortune 100 and Fortune 500 companies that for whatever reason, do not feel that they should pay equal pay for equal work. It is not happening everywhere, but where it is happening it continues to be startling.

Dell paid 9.1 million dollars to settle a gender discrimination lawsuit. Their suit claimed that Dell "systematically denied equal employment opportunities to its female employees" in compensation and promotions, according to the complaint. The company discriminated against women in training, in assignments of positions outside the U.S. and in programs designed to accelerate advancement, the complaint said. The complainants said that Dell had, "not only created a glass ceiling, but they had created a cement ceiling by which no woman could pass."[2]

Bethany A. Williams

In the pages of this book I share stories that I've encountered that may be like your own situation or that of someone close to you. I'll educate you on where you can find information to fight your own battle against the corporate Goliath to increase your pay to marketable rates, and I'll attempt with every effort in me to convince you why you owe it to this generation of women and future generations to come to gain the knowledge and use it to propel women's incomes forward, starting with your own.

By banding together and using your individual efforts combined with a team, you can change this by committing to getting yourself paid right. This is about a movement that starts with your salary and spreads to the women in your circle, then your distant friends and, eventually, around the world. This is about starting a grass roots effort where we take control and make change one woman at a time. You have to take action. You have to fight your wage battle. In doing so, you will propel the cause of women going forward for generations to come. This is the beginning of your stand.

This is the most important business book that you as a woman will ever read.

Fear of success: The bogeymen of politics, self-doubt, and pressure are keeping you from the money you deserve

Let's put on the table exactly what is holding you back and what you need to do to break away from it. Let's tackle the obstacles that obstruct your increased pay. First, let's discuss gender differences in the workplace.

3 Days to a Raise

In general, a larger percentage of men in the workplace seek money, position and power. These are not bad things and they certainly reflect the nature of men. There's also nothing wrong with women pursuing the same goals. However, if you are like many women I talk to, you feel more comfortable in a nurturing role. Winning is probably not your number one priority. You are not driven solely by a need to be in first place and earn immense amounts of money like the men that surround you. You seek recognition, and freedom, and a chance to impact your world. Nurturing is natural for you. Therefore, you tend to take care of those around you in perhaps a subconscious attempt to make the world a better place in the process.

Driven by an ability to persevere, you work to meet the needs of your children and family or yourself and are comfortable 'getting by'. Maybe you don't like change. Success to you is having adequately cared for those around you and worked a meaningful job where you received recognition. Maybe one of your biggest worries is being fired. Too scared to shake the tree and threaten the status quo, you shy away from true opportunities and hide, hoping that you have not threatened your role as it is today. You are loyal to a fault, worried about the company that you've nurtured, and living in fear of losing your job. You don't always believe in your own capabilities and strengths. These traits represent a position of weakness and are holding you back.

The result, albeit probably unintentional, is lower pay! By remaining in your comfortable sustainer role, you are potentially risking your job and holding other women back as well. You cannot negotiate for higher pay and better positions from this mindset or position. You can't make the working environment better for women from this vantage point.

Shift your thinking

It is time to shift your focus to leader thinking. This doesn't mean that you are selfish, it means you are empowered. You are the main one looking out for you. You have to be responsible for your interests, your career path, and your future.   It is okay to have a different agenda than the men or others that surround you at work. You can have a different motivation. Having a different agenda doesn't mean that you can't step to the forefront and be a leader. You can step to the front and make the world better for you, your family, and for women in the workplace.

Let yourself lead. Leading will allow you to help yourself as well the women coming up the ranks behind you.   Being on top makes it possible for you to make the work world a better place for women, single parents and others that don't fit into the mold of the workers that built the system that you now work in. Once in leadership, you can use your influence to change your company and the world around you. Companies with higher diversity in leadership make more money and achieve better results. You are holding your company back, and holding yourself and your pay back in the process.

I've done the same thing. I've spent years accepting #2 roles. I've fallen into 'follow' mode rather than 'lead' mode. I've let others set my path and paint my journey. If you want to make an impact, you've must take the lead.

3 Days to a Raise

This is more than just 'leaning in' to your career. This is about jumping in head -first and swimming completely under water. This is about setting a path and as you move up, taking the initiative to create positive impact, and allowing yourself the schedule freedom you need for a balanced life. This is about changing the definition of the leadership roles into something you'd like them to be, not the role you didn't want because of the hours or the politics. You are holding yourself back without proof that you can't do it and believing your own lies that the position must entail excessive politics, or that taking the role means you have no family life. Who says?

With more income will come a respite, a relief, and a reprieve that you can't yet imagine. Things get easier, not harder. You will be able to hire help to do domestic duties. You can spend more time doing the things that you value, time with your family, your passions and your special interests and charitable causes. Rising to the top will not be miserable. It will be amazing! What would you do with two to three times your salary? It is possible, and even realistic to attain. You will not attain it without a shift in mindset and a core belief that, *it's possible.*

Jump forward by starting with these three steps:

1. Make a decision to "do it"! Decide where you want to be, today, and take action before you talk yourself out of it.

2. Take action! Offer to help on projects, and lead in the role that you have. Choose to lead where you are regardless of your position or title. This is about creating an attitude of 'being in charge'. Ask about projects, positions, titles, and careers that you are interested in and

yearning for. Step out and apply for those positions. Why not?

3. Don't pause to think about it. Do not let fear hold you back. Fear only shows its power if you let it.

Set aside your fear, expose those faulty belief systems and constraints in your mind and chase after your new reality.

You could be making three times your salary. It is not only possible but also realistic. I want you to say aloud, "It is possible, and I'm ready to begin a journey into lands unknown. I'm ready to lead and chase after a new reality."

Why aren't you 'stepping up'?

What do you think keeps any population down? The absolute belief drilled into our minds that we are less than others and made to believe that our status has to fit into the norms and expectations of society. I'm asking you to break away from your acceptance of the norms and societal expectations and forge a new path. I'm asking you to stop sitting in the back of the bus.

Fear immobilizes you. It keeps you where you are, doing what you are doing and accepting the job and pay that you have. It is easier to do what you have always done and continue down the path that you are on. Any deviation from the path that you are enclosed-in seems, to you, like you are lost in the woods with no map. You don't want to change. You continue in as-is mode.

3 Days to a Raise

"Eighty percent of what we fear doesn't happen." Add up in your mind all the time and energy that you have spent worrying about things that never happened. You worry incessantly about unknowns that rarely occur. Your mind creates visions of the worst that can happen, and you stay stuck in a 'what if' analysis paralysis. Consider things in your career that you have not tried: promotions you didn't apply for, jobs you haven't taken, entirely new vocations that you didn't chase after, and raises you didn't pursue. You will not regret what you chase after, however, you will regret the components of your position, job and pay that you didn't seek out and run after.

Ever wonder what it would have been like to take that assignment overseas, or to move across the country for a job. Does fear keep you from moving forward? Don't let it stop you from making a move, wherever that move may land you. Follow your passions and take steps to achieve what you may currently feel are lofty and unachievable pursuits. You will accomplish some of the things that you pursue.

Mediocrity is your own worst enemy. If your job is good, but not exactly what you have dreamed of, you settle in and let it be. If it is horrendous, sometimes you will find the strength to make drastic changes to catapult yourself to a new level. Are you stuck in the middle? Are you living in black and white while dreaming of a vibrant highly paid career? It is time to add a little color to the palette of your job and stretch out of the fear that is immobilizing you.

Bethany A. Williams

How "Looking out for #1" doesn't equal being pushy, selfish, or tyrannical

Although women are getting more college degrees, more graduate degrees and entering the workforce at every level, you are holding yourself back. You make paltry excuses, such as, "I don't like politics", and you walk away from fantastic opportunities. It is time to change! Go ahead and take the role and decide to make it different. There is no, "This job has to be done the same way it has been done for centuries", sign on the office door. Decide to change things up. Take the position and make a concerted effort to do it your way, then see what happens. You would have made significantly more pay for the year you worked there. Risk more, push the envelope, and commit to change the game.

Your barometer is off. Not just for positions, but also for pay. When it comes to your job, you aren't assessing the correct value of your worth and you are underestimating what you are truly capable of. If a potential job sounds too hard, and the salary seems too high to you, you shy away and you don't apply. Today marks a change in plans, apply for that position and see what happens. Make a change and risk your comfort. Part of your inability to get the jobs you deserve and be paid what you are worth is a lack of acceptance of what you are truly capable of and what that dollar amount really should be.

This hesitation, this inability to pursue your own interests and higher-paying positions with a passion, is holding the system and each of us back from making positive changes for women, for our families, for changes in our salaries and, ultimately, a chance at a better life. Because you may not be driven by a pure competitive drive to be #1, you are

3 Days to a Raise

sliding into secondary roles and therefore #2 salaries, at best. You are openly accepting lesser roles and salaries and, as a result, are holding back progress for women overall.

The New Career Model- and How to make it Work for You

A new career model is emerging. As the economy has changed, so has how we maneuver our careers, our positions, and our pay. This new career model is about flexibility, innovation, and confidence. We see this new model at play in some industries and job types for example, in technology companies, entrepreneurs, lawyers, consultants, and accountants, have seen shifts in job function, schedule, and variation. In these emerging new models, women are moving up through the ranks, securing great positions and being paid well. Why? Because in these roles, woman can have 'mobile' offices. Woman can work unconventional hours, office wherever she pleases, work when she can fit it around her family and life, and more closely succeed at juggling her career to maintain a work-life balance.

As women are becoming subject matter experts, increasing in confidence and job skills, we see more requests for variations in schedule and demanding a," work on my time" schedule. What's emerging is women moving towards a new career model and a new way of work.

The new career model requires virtual collaboration: the ability to work productively, drive engagements, and demonstrate presence virtually. This virtual ability allows women to work at home after they've put the kids to bed, and work around a much more flexible schedule.

This new model has employees working on their computer, using Facetime or Skype to communicate with a co-worker in another office. This is already happening. In some industries it is a regular way of doing business, freeing women up to be virtual and allowing her to be 'present' for her family in ways not known since women entered the workforce in droves.

As tools evolve and technology continues to enhance, it is creating a workplace easier to maneuver for women. These virtual work forces make it easier to manage and become a part of an evolving career model that works for women.

You make life better for everyone; Believe it

Some companies are realizing that women in top management positions improve organizational performance. This has been well documented and companies have seen the benefits over time.

In the article by Adam Grant, Why Men Need Women published in The New York Times Sunday Review[6] he describes not only the financial benefits to organizations, but the whole host of indirect benefits companies receive as well.

> "We recognize the direct advantages that women as leaders bring to the table, which often include diverse perspectives, collaborative styles, dedication to mentoring and keen understanding of female

employees and customers. But we've largely overlooked the beneficial effects that women have on the men around them. Is it possible that when women join top management teams, they encourage male colleagues to treat employees more generously and to share knowledge more freely?   Increases in motivation, cooperation, and innovation in companies may be fueled not only by the direct actions of female leaders, but also by their influence on male leaders."

The new model requires you to speak up

The new work model requires women to speak up, catapulting themselves forward, suggesting themselves for raises and additional pay, and promotions, and volunteering to lead projects and teams. It requires a new comfort level at marketing your capabilities, knowing your strengths and being able to confidently speak up on the areas that you do well.

I often talk to women who have quit their positions, because they could not have the pay and schedule that they needed to accommodate changes in their family life. They gave notice, and walked away from their careers. Those who came to me before they quit, were introduced to a shocking new idea. Write up the schedule and pay that you'd require to keep your job and that would work successfully with your family life. Design a unique solution that gets the work done and matches to your unique needs to fund your family. Take that proposal to your manager. Go in with confidence, assured that your skill sets are worth it. If needed, propose fewer hours and less pay. Then, wait for an answer. What in the world do you have to lose?

Those who've done this have kept their jobs and been able to facilitate a better life. They have moved the ball forward, confidently realizing that it wasn't all or nothing. They realized that they didn't have to give up so easily. They struck forward with confidence they didn't feel, and charged ahead despite fears and reservations. Surprisingly to them, they succeeded. They were able to get new schedules and new arrangements that made it possible for them to achieve.

Quietly waiting to be 'discovered', or for things to change is a product of the past. This new work model necessitates that you speak up. Break out of your comfort zone, and march forward with brazen confidence in yourself and your abilities.

The ability to speak up, advocate for yourself, and ask for what you deserve may not be something that you do naturally. You get uncomfortable with being outspoken or fearful that you will seem over-confident. You are worried about over promising and under delivering. Don't be worried. It is a new world and we are operating under new rules. This is a new game and it requires different actions. This new world requires you to change.

Why you think this way: A peek at the cultural roots of your female behavior

During World War II the percentage of American women who worked outside the home increased by 11%, from 25% to 36%. More married women, more mothers, and more minority women suddenly found more jobs than they had

3 Days to a Raise

before the war. Instantly women were working jobs never before held by women and it was not only acceptable, it was necessary.

Because of the absence of many men who either joined the military or took jobs in war production industries, these women moved outside their traditional roles and took positions in jobs that were reserved for only men until that time in history .It is as if they 'suddenly' were capable, where only a short time before they were viewed as not.

Propaganda posters with images of "Rosie the Riveter" promoted the idea that it was patriotic, and not unfeminine, for women to work in nontraditional jobs. "They needed women to step up to the plate, and so, it was not only acceptable, it was requested. If you've used an electric mixer in your kitchen, you can learn to run a drill press," urged an American War Manpower Campaign. One example comes from the American shipbuilding industry. Women had been excluded from all jobs except a few office jobs before the war, yet women's presence scaled to more than 9% of the workforce during the war. As acceptance and attitudes changed, markedly, so did women's apparent 'ability' and skills to enter the workforce. It is as if women needed permission and with permission, it was then suddenly possible.

During this time in history, the game changed and it was okay for women to work in jobs that previously had been considered untouchable, unacceptable and just not right. The game changed for a time. Even though it was fine during wartime, when the men came back, they took over again and women were shushed back into our homes. We accepted the changes and moved back into our previous roles, forgetting what was possible and accepting the status quo. Slowly over time, women recaptured their sense of independence and began to strike out into positions again, this time not waiting for permission.

The game changed and it is changing again. This time, the culture is shifting to meet the needs of a flexible, dynamic, remote workforce who doesn't work the way it did in the 20th century, and which doesn't rely on or require structured in-office time. In this evolutionary new model, you need to know and be vocal about your strengths and capabilities, and press forward for positions and projects that fit those skill sets.

DAY 2: RESEARCH & LEARN: The 11 New Rules for Getting Paid

Rule#1: STOP Protecting Others More than Yourself

You're working against your own interest, by not advocating for yourself in the workplace for the money you deserve. Don't get me wrong, you are amazing at fighting for other's interests, just terrible at doing the same for yourself. If I put you in a room with a woman that needed to have her skills defended, you would come through for her like a champion, explaining the 101 reasons why she deserved the raise or promotion or deserved to keep her job. You'd deliver an Emmy-award-winning performance that would help her to keep her job. I'd be in awe of your abilities to defend her worth and fight for her value. You'd be able to remember the stellar accomplishments that have provided immense value to the organization. Now, turn the tables and pull up a seat. You are alone in that same room in front of senior executives and ask to defend your own position. I predict the room would get very quiet. You'd have nothing to say. You'd grasp at straws and stutter without ammo.

You'd struggle uncomfortably at positioning your skillsets and defending your worth. You'd be uneasy, unsure, with an unsteady and unconfident voice. The same woman, you, who fought for a co-worker is ill-equipped to confidently defend your own value and justify your own worth. You feel uncomfortable at using affirming statements emphatically professing your skills and strengths. You feel weak in the knees. Moments ago when you were defending someone else's worth, you felt confident and in-charge. Now that it is you, you feel on the spot and uneasy. Why is this? What part of our culture and environment has paralyzed you to fight for your job, defend your value\, and strike forward, with the same confidence you had to defend others? I'm not sure, I have however, witnessed this conundrum in countless situations. It is an epidemic.

Acknowledge your inability to fight for your own interests. This is a great first step to recovery. Fighting for your own interests doesn't make you selfish or proud. Ensuring that you keep your job, receive promotions and additional pay and defend your worth, it doesn't make you tenacious or a "brat". It, instead, is a mandatory requirement in this new market and new career model. Fifty years after the signing of the Equal Pay Act, we need to recognize that if we truly want to receive the positions and pay that we deserve, it means that we MUST be able to defend our worth and justify our value.

This didn't come naturally for me. I struggled through corporate life, hoping that if I just worked hard enough, I could attain higher positions and additional pay. I remained silent when I accomplished targets at work and sat quietly hoping that someday, someone would notice my results and promote me with additional pay and benefits.

It didn't happen. Instead, I watched those around me get credit for things I'd done. I saw others get promotions and additional pay. I realized that by not taking credit for the milestones and targets that I was achieving the 'credit' was going to others on my team and others in my direct reporting structure. People were being recognized. Promotions were definitely happening. Pay was definitely doled out, it was just not being paid to me.

By not being vocal, I was enabling others the opportunity and creating the perfect circumstances for them to receive the credit, pay, and promotions for work that I'd done. I remained a silent participant in a game where no one knew I had a player on the board. In retrospect, it is quite alarming to me to think of how much money I left on the table all those years. I am astonished by how easy it was to sit by and enable others to cash in on the rewards of my hard work and efforts. I enabled others to reap my benefits. I sat silently watching others succeed on the merits of my work. Are you doing this?

Once you recognize this characteristic, if it exists in you, you are able to rehabilitate your mind and recover from the addiction of selflessness. By denying yourself credit, attention, and recognition, you have held yourself back from making the money that you could be making. You have protected others more than yourself and in doing so, you have paid for their houses, cars, college tuition, and retirement funds while you sit in need.

Pursue Career Success & Your Values with a Passion

Success truly arrives and the money increases when you are free to let yourself pursue career success with a passion. This includes not only pursuing additional pay, benefits, and vacation time, but also allowing yourself to play as hard as you work; by not feeling guilty for taking time with your family and participating in family activities and key events.

At one point in my career, about 12 years in, I decided that I would pursue family time and personal achievements with the same passion and drive that I pursued work interests. I decided that life was short and that I was going to take all the vacation time I was afforded and live life to its fullest. If I was fired for that, so be it.

Seven years running I took my vacation time, pretty sure that I'd be fired upon my return. In reality, the constraints I felt were merely a figment of my imagination. I had dreamed up a self-limitation that was stealing fun and excitement from my life. Are you doing the same thing? I had imagined that I couldn't do such, and therefore, in my head it had to be true. Do you do that? I pushed myself through, continually telling myself that if I were fired, then that wasn't the right job for me. Now don't get me wrong, I had many a boss who said that I took more vacation time than they did, to which I'd respond, "Let me help you with that. How about I help you plan a getaway with your spouse." (I actually did help plan vacations for more than one boss, on more than one occasion.)

Bottom line: You are very likely holding yourself back by believing in some self-imposed rule that, in reality, does not exist. The flip-side to that reality is that doing what you feel is right for your family, your life, and your happiness will not have the negative impact at work that you think that it will have.

In fact, when I began to take the time I had earned, and treating myself better, I started to make more money. Surprised? I was too. Knowing that I could take vacation time, and that my worth and value would increase in my absence because no one was there to do what I do, gave me a heightened sense of purpose and value. In finding my power and voice, I realized my ability to fight for my worth. Fighting for time off had ultimately paid off (and actually has been easier than I anticipated with virtually no fight at all).

I suddenly felt empowered. I felt more valued. Being able to work hard all year and get away for two weeks in April, with no contact to work email, voice mails or the office, was incredibly empowering and satisfying.

My mind had time to think. I found my voice. I recognized my power. If it could do that, something that I never imagined was possible, what else could I do? The first several years, each vacation felt reckless. It felt criminal. How sick and twisted was my overachieving mind that I felt that taking vacation time that I had earned and deserved was somehow wrong or mischievous? I'd always thought that I was just strange for these feelings, but I've discovered that for a myriad of reasons, there are other women that struggle to 'let go' and take vacation time as well. Many feel 'tied' to their work. Some feel guilty leaving 'the office in a lurch'. Some just feel that it would 'look bad' or 'send the wrong message'. We need to develop a mind-set like the Europeans who have developed a culture of living life to the fullest and taking all their vacation time. In Europe, vacation time is, mandated, not just occasionally taken, but emphatically emphasized. It is no wonder their life expectancy is longer than ours in the United States.

Life is short. You will never regret the time you took off, the moments you found your power and voice and the time that you spent with your family. If only we could get the perspective of an 80-year-old , we'd quickly understand which priorities truly withstand the test of time.

Rule #2: Women; Assume you're (at least) 30% underpaid

Start by assuming that you are being paid 30% less than your market value. I know, that sounds high. But, starting at 30% undervalue is a great starting point. Statistics say that women are making, on average, 22-30% less pay. This is an average. Often times it is much higher than that. Did you catch that? *Much higher.* Think about that for a minute. At one point in my career I was making 200-300% under my market value and I had no idea. I am familiar with the concept of undervaluing skill sets because I did it for years. I underestimated what my skillsets were worth and I let others define my value. I worked for companies that grew quickly and, as a result, I ended up several hundred percent under my actual market value. I didn't know how far off my pay was. I had moved from a national leadership role to an international strategy role FOR THE SAME PAY, never giving it a second thought. I was simply happy that I had a job, working blissfully away, and silently falling far below my market value.

If you've been in the same company for longer than five years, have been in a growth company, or didn't negotiate your pay when you took your position, then you likely are being compensated 30% under your market value. I know you don't want to accept or hear this, but it very possibly could be true.

Let me share some stories

The reality of what is happening today with regard to women and pay astounds me. I've talked to many of you and heard your stories. You are not being paid what you are worth. You are under market value. When I hear the pay you are accepting and the work you are doing, it instantly elicits an increased heart rate and a higher blood pressure in me. You need to change it. Let's review stories from some of the women I've met.

Meet Denise. She is a manager at one of the Big Four accounting firms. She has been in a manager role for nearly six years, feeling stagnant, and not able to move up the ranks like she'd wanted to. At age 42, she was disappointed at her lack of progress. She hadn't ever pursued a promotion. But after reading two of my books, *Winning Strategies for Women*, and *Brand YOU*, she decided to take action. She then applied for and received a promotion to senior manager with a 13% pay raise. She was thrilled! She realized she wasn't stuck permanently and that she could realize her potential. She worked along happily for two years, and then she again paused to reevaluate. She had, after all, been logging more than 700 hours of overtime, time for which she was not compensated (which she knew). When she inquired about a director-level position, she was told she was not being considered for one. So, she started seeking out opportunities outside of the company. She quickly landed a director role at a competing firm—with a 67% raise to her base pay and an additional 30% in variable compensation. In one sweep, she doubled her salary! If you consider the 13% increase a few years ago, she raised her pay 110% in three years!

Nothing changed in Denise's world--except her attitude. Her perspective, belief, and actions took her where she is today.

Meet Jessica. Jessica has a job working for a technology company as an IT resource manager. Over the course of seven years, she received annual raises and four promotions. She enjoyed working there and got her certification in project management. Upon asking for a raise in her last review, she got only a very small percentage. She read *CEO of YOU* and decided to take control of her career. She started by doing market research and investigating her worth in the market. She quickly realized that she was far below her market value and so she began to seek other opportunities. When she interviewed for another position outside the company, she not only got a job at another company, but since she had researched her worth and documented her successes, she knew what to ask for. She had done her homework. She demanded higher pay, and as a result, she received a 70% raise.

Prior to doing the research, she hadn't realized how far below market value her salary was. With bonus potential, she will easily be making 100% greater income this year. WOW.! She jumped up and down at the sight of her first paycheck. She was working for a new company, but her title and responsibilities were exactly the same. She is now able to pay more into retirement, more on her house, and she will pay off car loans and a second mortgage within six months with money left over. She is working the same title and doing the same work; just for a different company. That is simply amazing. Could this be the case for you? You can start by assuming you are paid 30% below market value. Who knows what you will actually discover.

Even female CEOs of their own companies underpay themselves

This pay variance affects all verticals, industries, and all levels of female employees. Take the lawyer that attended my speech at the Lean In Group in Dallas. She negotiated for a $30,000 a year raise the day after she heard the speech on Asking for and Negotiating Your Worth. Prior to the speech, she had no idea that it was even possible. She was blissfully unaware of the possibilities. Do you think that describes some of you?

This variance also isn't limited to the women working for other companies. Women consultants that own their own businesses are not charging enough. Many estimate their fees, once they do market analysis, are determined to be 50%-100% below market value.

Even more shocking is women CEOs of their own companies aren't paying themselves the same way the male CEOs do, per the small business association. So, even when we select and pay our own salaries, we are undervaluing our skillsets at all levels.

Part of the problem is that you are under valuing your own worth. If you expect less, you make less. I'll walk you through easy steps to benchmark your pay and research your worth. The battle begins in your mind. Learn how to create a winning plan to catapult your salary and earnings to where they should be. It will start with learning to accept your value and using information you glean in your research to negotiate higher pay. You will learn to demand more; more raises, more promotions and more benefits.

Your husband is right, Your view of pay is all wrong

It's true, and I agree with him: You are underestimating your value on all levels. When presenting at a national women's conference a few months ago and asked the audience, "How many of you have fought with your husbands on how much you make and that you should ask for a raise?" Every married woman raised their hand.

You know why they aren't asking for a raise even though their husbands are begging them to? Women, in general, do a fantastic job advocating for their employers instead of themselves. They say, "You don't understand, we just had layoffs, they don't have enough budget, I can't ask for this or that." And the husbands aren't having any of it. And it spurs more after-dinner arguments than unfolded laundry and toilet seat positions combined.

You may not want your husband to be right, but moreover, you don't want to do something that's uncomfortable. And you certainly don't want someone telling you every night that you should do it. You might be able to avoid it at work, but, let's face it, there's no avoiding your husband.

What do men innately know that women just don't understand? They have these three things:

- a practical viewpoint of value/pay,
- an easy ability to put their interests first to protect and care for their family and themselves,
- and an understanding that to get a raise, you must ask.

They, of course, believe that asking doesn't make you pushy or too assertive. They see the world differently than we do, and their varying view is getting them more money and better positions and has for over 50 years. It is time to look at the world differently to change the paradigm and shift the curve.

Start seeing the world the way men do

It is time to start seeing the world the way your husband does--and the way men do. It is in their nature to confidently face challenges, whatever they may do. They do so with no apparent effort, and we could learn a few lessons in confidence from them. If things go well, they attribute that success to their specific skillsets. For you, when things go well, often you attribute it to luck or to your 'team'. This repeated reinforcement of their value, helps them to see their strengths and believe in their capabilities. With that belief, they feel confident to negotiate for higher pay. We give away credit and end up with a lacking confidence in ourselves.

If you are assuming your performance is related to luck, then you are robbing yourself of valuable confidence-building activities and, rather than reinforcing your value, you are further chipping away at your self-esteem.

You might think your spouse (or boyfriend or male friend) wants you to seek a raise for selfish reasons. Convinced that he wants you to ask for a raise, to better his circumstance or meddle in your affairs. Doubtful. Men have an indelible discernment about these things that women do not. They don't give up, and that is why men get raises. You'd rather just keep working hard and not bother with the incessant issue of whether or not you are being paid appropriately.

Rule #3: Don't Confuse Self Doubt with Reality

Occasional self-doubt happens to the best of us; however, you cannot allow those doubts to rule your world or define your reality. The problem is, that's exactly what they're doing--and you're letting them take over.

This journey to the land of YOU is about trusting your core strengths, focusing on the successes of your past, and driving forward with blind ambition and strength. Be the voice inside your head that says, " I can do it, I can do it, I can do it," rather than, "I can't, I'm no good, they are right, I'll never _____." Positive self-talk can overcome self-doubt.

Use facts and experiences from your work history to bolster your self-confidence. Think back over the career moments that you are most proud of. Document the things that stand out in your mind. If you felt amazing when you experienced or achieved particular work experiences, then you probably excelled and created superior results. Review and remind yourself of these facts. It will work to bolster your self-confidence.

Remember Your Successes

You have easily forgotten the great things you've done. Recognizing what you've done well is not bad. Acknowledging your value is not a negative. Openly accept this exercise to level-set your professional thinking.

Your end goal is to focus more on the facts of your accomplishments, not how you felt about them. Your value isn't about whether or not you felt valued. Your value is tied to actual results that you have achieved at work. Your value is tied to projects successfully completed, relationships created, deals closed, balance sheets balanced, etc. Your value to a company is about results not about whether or not you feel valued. Focus more on the facts and less on the feelings.

Case in point: A woman I coached in Dallas had won Dealmaker of the Year in commercial real estate. A very big deal, and a very prestigious award. But she didn't include it on her LinkedIn profile. When I asked her why, she said she didn't "feel" that there were many great deals that year. Do you realize how crazy that sounds? It doesn't matter how she felt about it. The award was a fact. And she had drowned it in feelings.

3 Days to a Raise

Stop finding ways to discredit your own successes and achievements. Claim them and promote them regardless of how they make you feel.

Action Step: List Your Successes

Get out a sheet of paper. Start writing the tales of your success. What amazing things did you do that you think of often? Write them all down, one by one, and don't stop until you've filled a couple pages. If you're having troubling thinking of something, think through past employers one at a time to spark your memories. Categorize your successes into success categories. These tales of your success are the confidence builders that you will use NOW and over the next few years to keep reinforcing to yourself that you indeed have high value. These tales of your success are your spinach to your Popeye arms and they will feed to your brain as well. Think super plump. I want you to keep writing until you think, "Wow, I've done all those things. That is simply amazing." Impress yourself. Keep writing until you are astonished with what is on the paper. Even consider building yourself a collage of your successes to post in your personal office space or place where you dress everyday. It is time for you to become your own cheerleader.

Make Your Memories of Your Successes Long and Your Failures, Short

For some reason, you remember every time that you failed. Those failures pound on the inside of your brains and cause intense havoc. When you've experienced failure, your soul lands in the doldrums and you feel the sting of disappointment. You cannot imagine how this could have happened to you.

Some of the best successes in the world have followed the biggest failures. Your failures pave the road to your success. You learn more, grow more, and refine your character more when you fail. The bigger you fail, the more you learn. You won't make that mistake again! It is an educational journey. It is like getting a certificate for a course completion. You've earned an education in that particular failure. You've learned more about creating success from that failure than any class that you could have taken.

What do you think of when you hear the name Abraham Lincoln? Do you visualize an amazing president? Or a failed businessman? He lost an election for state legislature, and at one point had a nervous breakdown. He failed as a farmer. He was finally elected to the legislature and he lost the vote to be Speaker. He ran for Congress and lost. He ran for the U.S. Senate and lost. He even ran for Vice President and lost. He learned from his failures. He didn't think that he was somehow less of a man because of his failures. He didn't then convince himself that those failures defined him. He didn't think that now, having failed so many times, that there was no way he could lead the entire country. No, he didn't. He didn't let his failures mark him a failure.

Are your failures blurring your vision? You can still be amazing at work, get that promotion, and achieve higher pay. Stay focused on results and the goals that spell results. Normally, you get careless and stop doing the things that you know you have to do to succeed. You start to spend more time listening to the noise around you and you are captivated by the constant movement of activities at work.

You must continue to do the right things, go through the right motions, and side-step the thoughts and activities that are drawing you away from your coming success.

Keep getting up. Higher pay lies in your ability to keep getting up over and over again. Everyone gets knocked down. They rarely talk about it. You are not alone. You are not the only one that has been knocked down. Keep trying. Don't take yourself down for the count. This work journey is about how many times you get up, not how many times you've been knocked down.

Pick yourself up, brush yourself off, and head in the direction of success and higher pay. It doesn't matter that you've failed. It doesn't matter that you've had a setback. You cannot give up trying, you cannot give up searching. You cannot give up. Period.

Failure is actually a prerequisite to your success.

Failure Better Prepares You for Success

Failing doesn't mean that you suck. In fact, you're mistaken if you believe that avoiding failure will minimize self-doubt. The best people, the brightest, the most successful, fail. It's a bridge you must cross to get where you're going. Self-doubt neither predicts nor helps you avoid failure. Nor does it mean you're doomed to fail infinitely, even if you feel it will. Every failure is a plank on the bridge that takes you toward success. It's what helps you learn. Self-doubt teaches you nothing. You may shy away from your failures and try to push them far from your mind, but failure is an important lesson in learning. It is the predecessor to success.

In failing, you learn more than you do in mediocre successes. You learn what you do not want to repeat and you dig deep to explore why it happened. The process of retrospective evaluation and analysis prepares you for a better path the next time that you cross that same intersection.

Don't be afraid of admitting to a failure or a weaknesses. Be afraid of NOT admitting to a failure or weakness and letting it grow and turn into your Achilles heel. You may feel that you simply cannot admit to any failures. Well, like it or not, you MUST. It is the only way to solve these and move forward.

You cannot avoid failures if you truly want to achieve the most success. You cannot avoid admitting mistakes or errors you've made just because you believe that you are better off not mentioning them. The company, and you, suffer by you not mentioning them. Put yourself in the mindset of the CEO. This is not about how you appear to your peers, it is about forwarding the companies initiatives and moving your career and the company forward. It is about what you've learned from your failures, not the fact that you failed.

It is a bit like having an addiction. If you cannot admit your failures and areas of weakness, than you will never attack them or solve them. If an addict refuses to admit his/her problem, the problem will live on forever. Problems do not go away until you embrace them, acknowledge them, and decide to change them.

Failure is not the end of your career. You know what is? Having a string of mediocre successes. You may not believe this, but you learn infinitely more from a huge failure than you ever do from a so-so success. Coming out of a significant failure causes you to re-think. It helps you orient yourself to performing much better next time. However, you don't have to experience the big failure to accomplish the same motivation. You can commit to making a difference and commit to not beating yourself to a pulp every time you do fail. You can be open to taking risks and pushing forward despite possible failures.

The rules for making money mandates that you take risk. Without launching forward with an adventuresome spirit and selecting choices at work that include risk, then you settle into a job and pay that has no pulse. Risk is uncomfortable. You shy away from it because you are more comfortable in an environment where you risk nothing. If you risk nothing, you gain nothing. Greater risk equals greater reward. Your pay will not reach the pinnacle of the mountain without your willingness to take risk. Start slowly, encouraging yourself to take little risks until you can move up the risk ladder to increased risky choices. With your heightened risk taking choices, your pay will climb. Risks are a necessary part of succeeding and creating opportunities for you to make the most money. To be paid the most, you must be willing to take risks and sometimes fail.

Learn Your Strengths to Catapult Your Pay

In order to catapult your pay, you need to know the strengths you were born with --- and use them. You are uniquely gifted with strengths that are different from anyone else's. These innate strengths power your passions and your abilities and make you unique. You may be well into your 30s or 40s and you may not yet know what your strengths are. The faster you can discover these, the faster you will increase your pay and find the silver bullet to catapulting your earnings.

What do you think your strengths are? Focus for a moment on the things that you most like to do. Think about activities that energize you. You will never tire of doing activities that fall into your strength areas; rather, you volunteer for them. They are what you like to do most of all. If you had a job truly utilizing your strengths, you would enjoy it greatly, you would do very well, and you would make more money doing it. Your goal is to understand your strengths *so well* that you strive to move into a position that uses those strengths on a daily basis—if you aren't already. This will be a key to making the most money that you can make.

Competition from others becomes less noticeable when you are utilizing your strengths. You have a gift in these areas. Find the strengths within you and use those strengths to propel your salary up.

Elizabeth, a mentee, was able to identify her strengths by listing out the projects or activities that she had done in the last five years that she enjoyed the most. By reviewing the list, she was able to determine the similarities and characteristics of those activities. They had a common theme of leading and organizing projects, aka project management. Each of the activities that she enjoyed doing resulted in her ability to see the results. They also involved interaction with the customers and speaking in front of groups. By evaluating the similarities and characteristics of her most liked activities, she was able to get an idea of her core strengths. Moving into a career path more focused on her strengths proved to provide her with a higher salary.

Knowing "what makes you tick," and understanding your unique gifts, are mandatory steps in increasing your pay. By focusing your effort and energy on your unique skillsets, you are driving towards the areas of you that would be the most beneficial to companies and, therefore, create focal areas in which you would most compensated.

Stop Blending in and Start Standing Out

I am a pioneer. While others dread change, I thrive on it. I prefer change. When faced with not changing or becoming the," victim of my circumstances", I much prefer taking on change. I like doing things a new way. I like driving change before it drives me. Combined with core leadership and speaking skills, and a passionate 'get-it-done' activator skillset, I have learned to find positions in companies that are created just for my unique gifts. I start new business lines within companies. I create divisions and services or products that didn't exist or grow market share by targeting new target markets. I am a growth agent. I love creating solutions that create market disruption. My corporate positions play exactly into my core strengths, but that hasn't always been the case.

Early on in my career, before I understood my strengths, I worked in and competed for standard leadership roles running departments. The competition was stiff, and my skillsets 'blended in' with the others. I was doing the job, looking around at how others were doing it and following their lead. I didn't take into consideration how my unique skills could add value for the company in that role. I didn't flavor the role and do activities in that role that I did well, so I looked just like everyone else. I didn't stand out. My role models were men, and I tried to duplicate what the men did, afraid of standing out and being different.

When I discovered my unique skillsets, competition became less of an issue. I wasn't looking to just 'run a division or a department', I was looking to build one. I used my unique capabilities to grow people and invest in talent and the development of my staff. I networked to discover where the best talent was and used connections to get to know them. I encouraged the teams I ran and created well-bonded teams that had great morale and sense of purpose. Together we developed a culture that was fun to work in and had a family like atmosphere. To my customers, I took on a 'family values' brand. I'd invite a man to a business dinner and ask him to bring his wife or invite a man to a professional basketball game and ask him to bring his son. I created memorable events that included their family and got a lot of business done in the process. I soon became a leader creating amazing results. I stood out.

Some call me the 'Golden Girl', saying that everything I touch turns to gold. When I stopped trying to be like everyone else and worked hard to figure out what made me different, and then applied those differences to benefit my employers, that is when the magic happened. It gave me an opportunity to stand out. Your goal is to so uniquely understand your core skills that you can carve out a particular niche for yourself that creates market opportunity for you. In your strength area, you are looking to be paid very well for having a unique hard-to-find skill.

The closer you evaluate and understand your strengths, the better your chances at differentiating your unique strengths and becoming 'in demand for what you do amazingly well. You also must become adept at marketing yourself in this niche area.

Rule #4: Sitting Back in Silence Won't Get You Ahead

No one will ever bring the raise to you. If you are sitting in silence, you will continue to do so because they are not going to march to your desk, lift you onto a pedestal and carry you around the office highlighting your accomplishments and culminate the experience with a fat bonus check and a raise. Wake up.

The top three reasons that no one will ever bring the raise to you:

1) Raises go to the people that are demanding them. Companies have a limited budget and cannot hand out raises to everyone across the board. They have to selectively give raises to the high performers, and to those who are threatening to leave but are irreplaceable.

2) Many companies feel, "if it ain't broken, don't fix it". If you haven't expressed a desire for more pay, and all is going well, it will stay as status quo.

3) Businesses are in business to make a profit. The more they pay you, the less they make. Their leaders are paid to make sure the company makes a profit.

You might believe that they know what you are thinking and what you need and desire at work. After all, you explained in detail what you wanted when you were hired or at your last review. You think they remember. They are so busy that they might not even remember your discussion about your needs. You need to lay them out frequently. Executives are focused on the biggest problem in front of them, and hopefully that isn't you.

From childhood, young girls are taught to "wait for him to call', so, initiating "the call" might feel uncomfortable. Without even realizing it, you might be thinking, "He'll remember what we talked about in my interview." Well, he may not. He may have an entire department or company to run and you are but a small piece of it. Senior executives in today's market are so overrun with information, that chances are very good that they cannot recall all of it. You'd have to remind him. You'd have to clearly state your expectations, which could make you uncomfortable. Your goal is to provide irrevocable value, make sure you are noticed and recognized for that value, and then communicate your needs in such a way that they feel compelled to give you a raise or additional benefits and pay.

The Waiting Game Doesn't Work

I worked for years, thinking that if I just worked hard enough, my superiors would recognize my hard work and promote me and give me additional pay and benefits. I suffered in silence, not asking for a raise and not applying for promotions. It didn't work. Even though I was working hard and achieving results, few knew of my successes. My immediate supervisor, although she knew of my successes, would have had to hire and train someone else if I left my position. The one person that could push me forward was in a position to directly be negatively affected by me getting a promotion. It would have been a win/lose. I may have gotten a promotion and additional pay, but she would have lost the 'best worker' she'd ever had, or so she said.

Years into my career I began to recognize that I was the one responsible to drive my career forward. That this bus wasn't moving unless I put it in gear and put the pedal to the medal. Waiting for action would not yield success. I had to create action. I had to take the steps necessary to drive the positions, and the pay. I had to ask for raises. I had to propose additional financial incentives and continue to be persistent until I was successful. You cannot suffer in silence to get ahead. You have to take action. You have to create the steps necessary to drive your pay forward. If they have a chance, they will underpay you. You have to demand the pay raises and persistently seek the right pay.

Use Skillful Manipulation to Get Your Raise

Women have been manipulating men since Eve persuaded Adam to eat the forbidden fruit. If you understand the psyche of your boss, and what it would take to persuade him or her to give you a raise, then apply that cunning and careful craftsmanship to achieving your pay raise. Why not? Sometimes alternating gentle and kind manipulation with direct requests backed up with quantifiable results will get the ball through the end zone.

You don't do it. You don't directly strategize, plan and go after your raise. It is easier for you to work hard and hope that the pay will come than to use skillful strategy, calculation, documentation, and carefully plan your request. You are not only fighting a culture that has taught you to take a back seat, but also by nature you often prefer to remain quiet rather than apply pressure to achieve your results. It is OK to use your natural abilities to subtly coerce combined with direct requests to get you the pay raise that you deserve. Stop feeling guilty about what you need to make you whole. Go and ask. Do it.

Rule #5: Taking Less Money Makes You Worth Less

It is true, if you make less, you are worth less. You think you're doing your company, your boss, your manager a favor by not asking—that you're saving them money, proving that you're invested in your work and aren't just "in it for the money." Wrong. So wrong. I'll introduce a few sad facts in this section; no one will ever tell you this, but the real truth of the matter is that the less you are paid, the less you are valued.

It's just how it works: People value what they pay for, not what they get cheap (which is why the purse you bought at Target is collecting dust at the bottom of your closet and your Coach bag sits on a high shelf). Not only does it affect you where you are, but it also will hurt your future prospects. If you're underpaid, companies with whom you'll seek employment will assume that you are worth less than you are. Being underpaid has marked you for future underpaying jobs. When you take less money, you are making yourself worth less. I agree that this truth is discouraging. It works both ways though, once one company pays you a lot of money, the next company is much more apt to do the same. You will have set your value higher ,then getting it again becomes much easier.

I've often 'proven' my worth to companies I've interviewed with by faxing them W2s from my last employer. What am I telling them? I'm showing them my value. They know that when a company is willing to pay me that amount, then I am worth that amount. Since I'm in a high wage category, this plays in my favor, but it works against you when you are being vastly underpaid.

Often I coach people who are vastly underpaid to skirt the issue of 'how much' they are making today. Use phrases like, for instance, "I wouldn't leave this job for less than X." Your position is worth more than your salary. You may have more job security where you are, or better benefits than a riskier endeavor that you may pursue. It may not be worth it to leave for less than a big jump if you are taking a big risk. I deter you from saying what your salary is if you are vastly underpaid. It could eliminate you from the search, even if you have the skills and qualifications.

Lower Paid Employees are Considered 'B' Players

If there are four of you in similar roles, and you are making the least of the four, the assumption at the top could be that the others are better at what they do. You and I both know that this may not be the case at all. The others could have been hired in after you, and done a better job of negotiating starting pay and raises along the way. But, nonetheless, the company executives will assume that the ones being paid more are better at what they do.

I've seen circumstances where women that were being underpaid, by companies that went out of business, were unable to find a new job because their wage was so low that the interviewing companies did not believe that they performed the job that they were purporting to have done. The next sad fact; NOT fighting for your value could be a risky endeavor. You may think that not fighting for the correct salary is the safer way to go, but I'd like to debunk this myth. Being low paid doesn't mean that you are giving your employer a bargain. It also does not ensure your job security. I found this shocking in my personal career.

Your cost cutting, coupon clipping mindset is costing you money and job security. Companies don't seek bargains. They need to get the job done the best, most efficient way possible. They don't seek cheap; in their minds cheap isn't good. They seek to hire incredibly smart people that perform well that could create millions more on the bottom line. If they are going to cut corners, it will be in the low level positions, certainly not in leadership and at the top of the food chain. They want to hire in the best and brightest that are guaranteed to get the job done right. YOU are the only one thinking about getting your company a bargain. They are not bargain shopping and you do not want them to think of you as cheap or being at the bottom of the barrel. You want to be performance driven, valued, and priced market competitively.

Having a 'bargain' salary is not good for you or your company. If you think that you are 'flying under the radar' because of your 'low' salary, you actually are doing just the opposite. You are showing up on the radar, all right, but as the lowest or a lower-paid person. This puts you in position for possible elimination. You are creating an image that you are 'less' valuable and subjecting yourself to a possible reduction in force and, if you are laid off, finding another job will be difficult because you are so far under market value. Others will not believe that you actually did the job you are saying you did at such a low salary. You will be ruled out before you ever get to the interview.

The final sad fact; you think you are protecting yourself, when in reality, you are risking it all.

Rule #6: Be the CEO of Your Career

Your career path, jobs that you have access to, your network, and the opportunities presented to you rest entirely on your shoulders. You are responsible to manage your career path and your earnings.

This new job market and economy has brought with it monumental shifts that, translated, means that *your role has irrevocably changed!* It hasn't always been this way. The average worker will change jobs every two to three years and have more than 26 jobs in a lifetime. Did you get that? You could have 26 jobs in your lifetime. It makes me tired just thinking about it.

Not that long ago, career paths and career management was the responsibility of your employer. It made sense for your employer to invest in their people, train them, and ensure that they were positioned properly to end up in exactly the right role to match their skillsets and capabilities.

Then everything changed. Seemingly overnight, average job tenures declined from 10 to 20 years to two to four years. Companies immediately shifted their focus to hiring the right talent, not, for the most part, growing their talent (ie., on-the-job-training). So, what does this mean for you? It has left YOU in charge of your career and career path.

You are now responsible to manage your career and maximize your earnings. You have become the CEO of YOU. *How will you ensure that you make the most money you possibly can?* What steps and plans will you put in place to catapult your capabilities, skillsets, and brand to the top of a very competitive global pile?

It is time to shift your thinking and begin thinking of yourself as a product. You own the rights to YOU. You are the CEO, chief marketing officer, chief financial officer, chief human resources officer, brand champion, asset manager, and stylist for you. You own the YOU Enterprise.

It doesn't matter if you are unemployed, or earning seven figures a year, or anywhere in between. Each one of you has a daunting task. How will you manage the assets of the YOU Enterprise? You will learn to be CEO of YOU, and better manage the opportunities before you.

When you need to help a friend or family member find a job, you do an amazing job at it. You defend her value and define a course of action. You are driven and focused. It is time to strike ahead, defending your value and setting a course of action with the same persistence and drive as you would for that of a friend. You need to look at this exercise as a mandatory precursor to success, not an optional step. In order to succeed and make the most pay, you MUST defend your value and create a great career plan that promotes you into the highest-paying positions, negotiates for the highest pay, and gets you on a different path.

Stop Letting a Faulty Belief System Hold You Back

You could have belief-system baggage that is holding your pay back and keeping you from making the most money. Belief systems, as described by British philosopher Stephen Law, "draw people in and hold them captive so they become willing slaves... if you get sucked in, it can be extremely difficult to think your way clear again." A belief system can keep you from achieving your full potential if you believe that success isn't possible for you, or that you aren't worth 'that much', etc. Whatever your faulty belief system is, it could be holding you back.

To expose your own faulty belief system, scrutinize YOU. Do you hold a faulty belief system, or a set of specific beliefs you are clinging to, like "I don't have time" and "I'm fine right where I am" , "I'd have to give up my family time if i took an executive role," etc.? Define those reasons that you use to rationalize not going for it, not moving ahead. That is the thing you want to fix.

Let's review some of the most common faulty belief systems. You may be caught in one of these traps. Read these with an attempt to self-identify any of these that apply to you:

Faulty belief #1: "If I fail, my career is over."
What it really means: You believe the worst possible outcome. You believe that possibly, maybe, or more

accurately most likely you are not capable of that position or role and trying for it will simply result in failure. To not embarrass yourself or have to deal with the feeling of being a failure, you choose to stay right where you are.

Why it's dangerous: Rather than recognize your contributions, building your confidence and taking risks, you are beholden to your fears. By letting fear drive you, you are missing out on valuable opportunities and losing chances to work challenging and exciting projects. Yes, you may fail, but your career will not be 'over'. You will have learned valuable lessons that will move you towards your next success.

Faulty belief # 2: "I make enough, I don't need to ask for more" or "Money can't make me happy", "I'm paid well enough, I should just be happy."

What it really means: Fearful of having to ask and risk rejection, you are rationalizing. You believe that you are not worthy of X pay. Perhaps you think that you aren't worth more than you are currently making. You are taking the easy way out. Rather than ask for a raise or a promotion, you simply rationalize 101 reasons why they shouldn't pay you more to avoid having to ask or try.

How this costs you: This belief keeps your wages lower than they should be. By expecting less, you demand less and get paid less. Although you don't need money to be happy, it is still your prudent responsibility to seek out and get the pay that you deserve for your skill sets. You'd call someone silly if they were selling a brand new Mercede

3 Days to a Raise

Benz for the price of a used Volkswagen. Value is value and your worth is your worth whether or not you accept that you deserve it. This is costing you pay raises.

Faulty belief system 3: "I've just been lucky." "My success has been driven by a few lucky shots that are not repeatable." "I've gotten where I am by pure luck. If I try to depend on that luck going forward, it will let me down."

What it really means:.   You believe that you got here by luck, and that means that you believe life happens to you— and that you have no hand in creating change yourself. You are discounting your successes and your hard work. You didn't get where you are by simply being lucky over and over again. You've worked hard and accomplished great things but you are taking away your own credit and robbing yourself of your power.

Why it's dangerous: This is a risky belief, because it takes you out of the driver's seat. It makes you the victim rather the person in control of your destiny. By believing that you are just lucky, you rob yourself of self-confidence that would normally build due to your success. You don't believe you've earned it, therefore others don't build faith and belief in you either. By discounting your success, you are much less likely to take risks and pursue your job passions. It causes you to sit back and wait to be lucky again rather than take action.

**Faulty belief # 4: "A promotion will cost me my life."
"If I charge more or make more, I'll pay the price elsewhere."**
What it really means: You are buying into a lie that is holding you back. If you accept a higher position, you are still responsible for your schedule and for making sure that you pay attention to your family the same way that you have to do today. You will actually have more flexibility and resources at your disposal. This is only true if you let it be true. You control your schedule and can create a circumstance where you have a job and a life.
Why it's dangerous: This belief holds you back.
Believing this keeps you from applying for promotions and additional pay. Without advancing, you are preventing an easier life for yourself, possibly keeping your children out of the best colleges, and holding back the cause of women everywhere.

Faulty belief #5: "I don't want to be disliked, or be seen as pushy or bossy." "I'd have to step on others and back-stab to get to the top."
What it really means: You have heard negative messages and you've bought into their validity. Global categorical generalizations are never right. Many women that take leadership roles are amazing, warm-hearted women that are changing history, making the world better, and helping their companies earn a better bottom line. You owe it to your company to help enable their success. I'm sure you've seen women backstab and hurt others, yet you can decide

that you're not going to do it. The choice is entirely yours. You do not become a different person just because you receive a promotion. You will be the same you. You choose the path and how you maneuver it. There is no one way. You can succeed without any dirty tactics at all.

Why it's dangerous: The same as faulty belief #4, this thinking holds you back and steals your power and your ambition. It is another excuse that you use to not push yourself forward where you should be.

Faulty belief #6: "I'd have to compromise my morals to get where I want." "People with special connections will always get ahead of me." "It's who you know, not what you know."

What it really means: You don't have to compromise your morals to succeed. You are setting back the course of progress for years to come when you believe such faulty beliefs. Companies want talented individuals that create results. They want to make a profit. They do not want you to make bad decisions that will negatively affect the company.

How it costs you: You settle into #2 roles, letting others with potentially less moral backbone than you, lead the company. You opt-out, de-select yourself, and lose out on challenging and exciting positions in the process.

One or more of these faulty beliefs may be holding you back from moving forward or you may have one that I haven't listed. Whatever is altering your reality, choose to rule out these beliefs. They are an accumulation of culturally enforced beliefs, often handed to us by parents and authority figures. That is why it takes more effort to overcome them. Similar to a fear, they can only hold you back if you believe that they can.

Unabashedly list your career and earnings dreams or goals. Write them down. Stare at them. Is there any part of you that believes that you are making your own excuses? Do you believe that you are not worthy of higher pay because of where you grew up, or that a salary sounds too high because of your surroundings or those that you've met in your life? Maybe you have never met anyone that made that much money. It is your responsibility to call out your faulty belief system(s) and convince the new you that these no longer apply. Strike-out convinced that nothing can hold you back from where you want to go and what you want to earn.

Highly Paid Equals Rightly Paid

You think the salary you deserve is probably too much to ask for, based on how you feel about it. But your internal barometer is way off, trust me. You could be self-denying yourself positions and pay because of a faulty misconception that your value is much less than it really is. High pay (to you) could actually equal right pay in reality. Your misperceptions could be holding back your pay. This is astonishing to think about, I know. But it is worth considering. Fewer females end up in high-level executive positions because we are asking too little in salary, and by asking too little, we look inexperienced and appear to be less qualified than those with the same experience and skills who are asking for more. We are creating our own limited experiences.

3 Days to a Raise

This is a drastic statement, I get it. But I've seen the reality of it play out time and time again. If you have defined goals and those goals are tied to a belief that you cannot make x amount, then it is time to redefine your goals to match to your NEW unrestricted belief system. It is time to set a new course of action. Set a higher goal, and define a different future and make it happen. If you set higher targets and miss them, you will still achieve more than setting low targets and hitting them. Convince yourself to start believing that the results are achievable and that certain actions could equal higher pay. It doesn't matter where you've come from, this is about where you are going. You are setting a course for a destination, a.k.a. a position that includes use of your distinct skills. Finding a position that utilizes what you are especially good at, for a company that you enjoy, will equal the highest potential pay. You can make more doing exactly what you are doing today.

Map out a few companies that you'd like to work for or a few positions that you'd love to have. You are now CEO of your career and your career aspirations. What would it take to get to where you'd like to go? Like planning for a long road trip, knowing the destination will help you to set your course.

Stop Being too Busy or using 'Busy' as an Excuse to Stop Strategizing

You need to start with a great plan. Your goal is to manage your long-term vision of where you'd like to go and be prepared to find and jump on opportunities along the way.

We often get busy in a role and close ourselves off to other opportunities. Managing your career and lifetime earnings will involve listening with an ear to the ground, always being aware of your need to stay focused on potential opportunities that could benefit you in your next possible role.

When you accept the status quo and get comfortable in your job, you stop strategizing and stop playing the 'advancement game' mid-job. You tend to focus only on success in that role. When you aren't focused on being two steps toward the door because the job is providing you what you need, you settle in and accept things as they are and you miss opportunities for higher pay.

Those who find themselves suddenly out of work, had gotten comfortable in their jobs. They never suspected their sudden 'exit' and are caught surprised and unprepared. You cannot afford to be caught surprised and you cannot let yourself be unprepared. Unprepared means that you are not managing your career well. Unprepared means that you are at the whim of your company and could be caught in a buy-out, leadership change, or sudden market change that leaves you with few to no options or, simply stated, it could mean that you are making less than you could be making.

Your attention needs to be both focused on your current position and your next one, since the next one could and will pay you more. Be prepared for a move and ready to negotiate a higher-paying next role. Being vigil and slightly focused on other opportunities on occasion will ensure that your interests are always protected and that making more is in your future.

3 Days to a Raise

But, how do you find the time? You can. You really do have the time. I am not talking about a new full time job. It is not about dedicating an intense amount of time to your 'watch for more money plan.' It is about *having* a watch plan. It is about an occasional discussion and focused attention on the goal. It is a thought process that dedicates *some* time to the possibility of another, better opportunity opening up elsewhere. Often it isn't just about discovering opportunities; it is about creating them.

Brainstorm Possible Paths to Success

A great skill to develop is the ability to brainstorm options and possible alternate positions and career paths in pure brainstorming mode. You may even try to convince yourself that you are thinking up possible paths for someone you know with skills exactly like yours, not for yourself directly. Refuse to allow yourself, initially, to rule anything out because of location, title, responsibilities, etc. Develop the ability to dream up possible paths you could take and a vision of your future, no matter what part of your career you find yourself in. Do whatever it takes to begin getting YOU to think about your future and alternate career path options that would pay you more.

What do you envision for your career in five or ten years? Have a goal in mind for your long-term path as well as a shorter twelve- month plan. It is time to map out a plan and investigate your options. Your company isn't going to do it for you and you've been limiting your opportunities by not doing it.

Rule #7: Don't Let Past Disappointments STOP You from Moving Ahead

Often when you don't get a raise, fail at a project, or simply hit a huge disappointment at work, you stop performing. You stop giving it your all. You convince yourself that you can't move forward, that you aren't good enough. Don't let past or current disappointments stop you from moving ahead. YOU MUST keep performing EVEN if you feel like you are underpaid. Keep moving ahead even if you think that all is lost.

Don't let your attitude suffer just because you have failed. You can't start to think that you can stop trying because you will 'fail anyways'. When you do that, you become less valuable to your employers, and you begin seeming less engaged, and less productive. Doing a crappy job because you are disappointed over not getting a raise, a project, or a new role will not get you ahead. I want you to outperform despite past failures. Do the job and work of someone making twice your pay, and someone who hasn't failed, and stand by, because soon you will be the person also getting paid more.

It is imperative that you continue to blow out the seams of your job and march towards the career and pay that you deserve. You are a brand. You need to rock it. Do a fabulous job and your pay will follow. You'll make sure that it does.

3 Days to a Raise

Drive Amazing Performance

Driving amazing performance and achieving stellar results will help support your ability to use those successes as you go forward to drive higher pay. Working hard and creating results that people notice will help you raise your pay if, and only if you use it as a quantifiable reason for you to get more pay when you go to the negotiating table. It creates the tools in your tool chest to get you paid more.

Why do you think your performance has fallen beneath amazing? You've probably lost steam. Maybe you want to believe that working hard will create more pay, but you've been doing it for so many years that now you can't imagine that it is going to work and that your circumstances will change. In your mind, you think, I know, I know, the definition of insanity is doing the same thing and expecting different results. I am not asking you to do the same thing and expect different results. Actually, if you don't combine it with the other steps, it won't. But, combined with the ability to ask, fortitude to seek out an exit plan, developing an incredible brand that makes others aware of what you do well, and then applying those skills at work will drive you to higher pay.

Rule #8: Know Your Value & Worth

I talk to thousands of people annually. I always start by asking them what they do incredibly well. I can immediately tell how successful someone will be in finding new opportunities or getting a raise by how they respond to that one question. When I ask , "Why do you deserve a

63

raise?" , silence is often the response. Can you answer that question? Begin to think long and hard about the value that you bring to the company.

Stop working inside the box of your job and work to provide value outside of your position, and use your core skills to contribute to the company's forward direction. You have a function, you fulfil a need that the company has for you to accomplish results. Providing more value will equal you making more money. You need to determine where you can provide the most value and then provide or add that value. You are there to achieve a set task, resulting in meeting committed goals at the highest level of the organization. Regardless of the type of role, or what level you are at, whether or not you further the goals of the company is of utmost importance. Upping your contribution to achieve more success and more results for your company will equal more pay for you in the future.

Would you pay a bill to XYZ company if you didn't know what the charges were for, what service was provided, or what value was received for the price? Doubtful. Not being able to provide immense value to your employer is a risky endeavor, and not providing high results is going to limit your earning potential.

Assess Your Contribution

Have you thought of how you are perceived in the workplace and within the various projects that you work on. Time is of the essence. Consider how you are spending your time. Are you productive at work? How are you perceived in the meetings that you attend? Are they productive? Are your projects completed on time and done well? If you are in sales, how promptly do you follow up? For leaders, do your employees love and respect you or shy away in fear when you walk by?

Carefully scrutinize your own work. Evaluate the work you do as if you were the owner or CEO of the company. Take a very critical eye to your attitude, your own work, and the relationships that you have or haven't formed with your co-workers, boss, and subordinates.

Assessment Activity Part I--- Self Evaluation:

Start by asking yourself these questions. Look critically at your performance and evaluate your worth.

- **Positive Impact/Results**

    - Do you encourage others towards success? Do you positively affirm them?
    - Do you ignite a positive, get-it-done attitude that permeates all of those around you to want to perform better, work harder, and be at the top of their game?
    - Or, on the other hand, are you dragging others down and pulling down the office productivity?
    - Are you liked or disliked at work?
    - Are you achieving the goals set for you?
    - What do your employment reviews say?

- **Appearance & Professionalism**

  - How do you look and dress?
  - Do you carry yourself professionally?
  - Does your look complement the company or do you drag down the standards?

- **Skillsets/Gifts & Talents**
  - What unique skills do you possess that you can use to grow the company, reduce expenses, build a better brand, or improve performance at work?
  - What problems at work are you uniquely gifted to solve?
  - Can you train or influence others to perform better?

If you have trouble with this self-assessment, you could always call your mother, sister, brother or other relative. Relatives often tell us the honest to goodness truth when others boldface lie.

Assessment Activity Part II--- Outside View:

Ask someone at work who doesn't like you or someone who recently quit to answer the above questions, they may be more honest with you. Write down the adjectives that come to mind. Make a list of what you think you do very well and areas that you need to improve. Stop thinking 'Why do I care?' and move towards 'I care and aim to improve'. This shift will be noticeable at work and will improve your value and chances at higher pay.

Ask Others to Identify What You Do Well

Now it is time to see what others say you do well. Knowing your strengths from other's opinions will help you to be able to articulate your worth. Locate five people that you either work with today or have worked with in the past.

Use Surveymonkey.com to get anonymous feedback to the following questions. Ask them to answer honestly and explain that it is anonymous, that you are working on a career path planning exercise and their honest answers are critical to the success of the exercise.

Explain in the survey that no comments will upset you. You need honest constructive criticism for this to be a successful exercise.

Dear _____,

Thank you for agreeing to assist me in my career path planning exercise. I need your honest input on the following three questions. This will help me to define a path forward and will give me a chance to understand both the positive and any negative aspects that you think of when you think of my work skills and experiences.

1)   I can always count on (insert your name) to :

2)   When I think of (insert name)'s work skills, what really stands out is her ability to :

3)   Characteristics that I think of when I think about (insert name) and her work are:

   a. Positive:

   b. Negative:

Thank you for your time and honest feedback.

This is of vital importance. This critical information will help you to understand how people perceive you today. It will also help you to understand positive traits that are reflected in your work. You will want to accentuate the positive and avoid worth and value statements that point to your negative characteristics. If you understand the positive characteristics that you possess, you can use those to capitalize on the positions and opportunities that maximize those assets. You can embrace the parts of you that are great, and then reinforce those positives to catapult your pay.

Learn to Easily Articulate Your Value

In order to make the most money that you can possibly make, you need to understand your assets and be able to easily articulate your value and worth. After you've thought through your strengths in Rule #3, take the strengths that you've identified and package them up with the best messaging and value and proactively sell them into companies looking to hire people like you. Even if this is difficult, do it. It's time for you to stand up for what you are worth.

Knowing your value and being able to apply it to the benefit of your company is a gift to your employer and future employers. If you know what you do very well, and you share that information, it will help to move the company forward. It is your obligation to help your company or a future employer to get the most profit and benefits out of the work that you do well. Own your strengths. Be able to articulate your value. Don't shy away from conversations about what you can do to further the profits or strategies of the company. Helping your company understand what you do well is your obligation. In volunteer organizations, you find it easier to speak up and tell the leader what skills you possess and how to put those skills to work for the benefit of the organization. It is easy for you to understand and comply. That task seems easy. But shift that same principal to work, and you may suddenly get weak in the knees at the thought of articulating what you do well. Don't over-analyze yourself, just learn to do it even if it feels foreign and awkward.

Remember that first kiss when you were young? It might have felt awkward because you were inexperienced at it. This is no different. As you practice this skill, like kissing, it will become second nature. You will not have to think about it and over time, it will become much easier to do it without feeling shy or awkward. Keep practicing, and soon you will be able to articulate your value and identify easily what you do incredibly well. As Albert Einstein once said, "If you can't state it simply, you don't understand it fully." Your employer and future employers need to know.

Rule #9: There is More to Compensation than Cash

When you think of compensation and pay, you think of salary. Your mind is stuck in the 'cash' department. You think about that check that is deposited into your bank account every two weeks. For the most part, you don't consider your total compensation package or benefits beyond salary. It is time to start thinking about the total picture. In your attempt to storm the bank and take the best withdrawal, you are leaving a ton of gold bars in the safe.

Because you're focused on salary, how you'll pay your mortgage, and what will be left over, you may be missing the forest for the trees. Other pay options are powerful ways to increase your wealth and they can go beyond compensating you--they can make you rich. Despite availability and propensity of these other options, they are not being awarded to those that don't ask for them. You won't get them if you don't ask. You can ask for them prior to starting a position, during your tenure, after accomplishing a major task, and any time during your employment. You may be thinking, "I wouldn't even know it they were worth anything." Getting a piece of a very small pie is better than not negotiating for any pie at all. It is always better to ask. It is always better to get what you can and determine its value over time.

Let's review some 'pay' options, in addition to annual salary and pay increases that could make you wealthy. You could make a fortune in 'other' benefits. Real wealth is made from these type of options. You can choose to live on an annual salary forever or you can read this, move forward with a new strategy and direction, and potentially choose to retire on a boat in the islands or wherever you

3 Days to a Raise

dream of retiring. Wealth begins and ends with something bigger than just your check every week and if you think this section is only for 'those' other people, you are wrong. This section is for each one of YOU.

Let's look at an extreme example. From 1986 to 1996, Microsoft's stock soared more than a hundredfold as the company's Windows® operating system and Office® applications dominated the PC industry. That explosive climb made millionaires of employees who had accepted options as a substantial part of their compensation. "While the exact number is not known, it is reasonable to assume that there were approximately 10,000 Microsoft millionaires created by the year 2000," said Richard S. Conway Jr., a Seattle economist whom Microsoft hired to study its impact on Washington State. Did you get that? Approximately 10,000 employees became millionaires by the year 2000 because they owned stock in Microsoft that they had received as a component of their pay. Some of those employees were secretaries and programmers. They are now millionaires. That could be you.

The IPOs of Zynga and LinkedIn created roughly $16.7 billion in market value. Usually 20% of the equity goes to rank-and-file employees as stock options. That would make the amount of instant wealth created to the employees, with stock options, more than $3.3 billion. Can you say, " WOW!"? Do you need more examples? *Or do you believe me that this is worth your time to evaluate, figure out and understand?* It is not as hard as you are making it out to be and it is certainly worth your time to try to figure it out.

Bethany A. Williams

Stock Options in Publicly Traded Companies

An option is literally that: An option to buy stock at a specific (and special) price, called a strike price. It's the "sale" price of the stock that only you and a few others have access to. Options are special SALE prices for a piece of the company, which allows you to get stock for a discounted price, which you can sell later for more. For instance, if you were offered a pair of Christian Louboutin for $200 instead of the retail value of $600, you'd have saved $400. If you could re-sell them as new, you'd make $400. In effect, stock options are sale prices on company ownership that you can re-sell and pocket the difference.

So if Apple is selling for $90 a share, the company can grant you an option that allows you to buy it for $20 a share. That's a steal. For each one stock option, you could make $70 a share if the stock price stayed the same. If it goes up, you can make even more.

Perhaps you are wondering why companies do this. Companies do this to:

    A) Keep valuable employees 'locked in' , ie, keep you from leaving (I'll explain this in a moment) and to
    B) Motivate you to help grow the company. The greater the value of the company, the greater your portion will be worth. If the price of the stock goes up, you keep all the increased value.

These options are given to you with the intention of keeping you at the company, so they don't let you sell them all at once. That wouldn't incent you to stay. These options 'vest' over a period of years. Vesting refers to how long it takes before you really own them. On initial grant, you get only a 'promise' of future options. You are allowed to sell a part of those options in the future as defined in your option letter. You could be allowed, for example, to sell 1,000 of the 5,000 options in the first year. In other words, they are only allowing you to access 20% of your options in year one with a vesting schedule that keeps you there five years before you can cash in all of the benefits of the options that they granted you.

These are often called 'Golden Handcuffs'. They refer to a company's ability to keep you at the company for a set period of time so that you don't take another position. They are betting on the chance that you will sit and wait for your options to vest. They payout is so great, that often employees will work hard and 'wait' for vesting to occur before they quit their position and move on to another company or another role. Each year as they' become vested', employees are able to sell the number of shares that they now own, or 'have vested'.

For example:
- Suppose you were awarded 5000 Apple options at an option price of $20 a share. In this scenario, you would make $70 a share if you sold them when they vested.
- If the price of the stock rises, you can make considerably more. It varies based on market value of the stock. Prices of the public stock is listed on the exchange that it is traded on. Many web sites allow you to easily pull up the existing value of a stock on any given day based on the Ticker symbol,

the group of letters that the stock is traded under. For example, Apple stock can be found using the Ticker symbol AAPL.

Any value above the price granted, you get to keep. If they award you a very high strike price, then they are not doing you any favors. For example, if the current stock is trading at $15 a share, and they offer a strike price of $30 a share, don't consider this much of an asset. The stock would have to double in value before your options would be worth anything. It is possible that the company stock price could grow that substantially, but certainly it is not guaranteed and it would take a long time.

These options will only be worth something if the company does well and the stock price increases, because you only make the money on the price above the strike price. They, and you, are betting on the success of the company.

The company hopes the stock price rises, as do you. If it doesn't grow, your options aren't worth anything. They could, for example, award you 5,000 options at the current 'price' that the stock is selling, or $90 a share. Today, they wouldn't be worth anything since the 'sale' price is the same as the actual price and you only make the money on the difference. That's the risk you take.

This enables the company to reward you if you are a major contributor without direct cash being paid out of their pockets. If you were to sell your options when the stock rises to $290 a share, then you pay the $90 a share back to the company, and keep $200 a share. In this example, $200 X 5,000 = $1,000,000. Those options would be worth a million dollars. This is how many employees working at company names that you know well have made their money. Think about Facebook, LinkedIn, Zappos, and the list goes on.

Options are more available at small- to mid-size companies, certainly much more difficult to obtain in large companies. Investigate to figure out your company's stance on options. When you sell your options is also important, but today I want you to focus on GETTING the options. We will focus on managing them later.

Gifting Stock/Public Stock Grant

Whereas a stock option is an option to buy that stock, a stock grant is a gift. No purchase necessary. Much like a gift card, it has cash value. Both are valuable, yet grants are always the nicer option because there is no pay-back for the stock. These 'gifts' are the company giving you a piece of ownership in the company as an added benefit.

Stock grants are used to incent you to stay, to work hard, and to help grow the company. It is to deter you from running away to another company at the first offer that you get for additional money. Some companies use stock options that we covered previously, yet some use straight out stock grants or gifts. These are usually reserved for higher level positions, but anyone can receive a stock grant. They are intended to vest over time, keeping you 'handcuffed' to the company so that you stay long-term to help it grow. Many of these also vest out over four to five years.

Never turn down either options or grants. You have nothing to lose. It is like gambling in Vegas. If someone else is buying your chips, let them. You might win big, but not playing means you are guaranteed to not win at all.

Private Company Stock

Private company stock can be a little more complex. If you accept a position with a private company, you'd get what's called common stock. If venture capitalists invest in that same private company, they'd get what is called preferred stock, which often comes with a guaranteed percentage on cumulative earnings. Their preferred stock will payout before your common stock. When companies calculate out the preferred interest rate dividend, or guaranteed payback, for the venture capitalists, there could be nothing left over for the common shareholders, even if you thought your stock was worth hundreds of thousands of dollars, you could be left with nothing. To avoid being left empty-handed, it is is important to understand the investment table, who owns stock in the company and what type of stock that ownership represents. Very senior executives have been burned before on this, simply by asking to review the investment table and not realizing that the Preferred Stock had a guaranteed percentage payout. If that is the case, there may be nothing left for the common stockholders. Common stock is worth more in a private company if there are no preferred stock shareholders. Ask to see the investment table and quiz them on the ownership of the company. It will help you to make a wise decision.

3 Days to a Raise

Performance Bonuses

Consider negotiating for a performance bonuses based on a goal in your area. These pre-defined cash bonuses can motivate you as well as help the company meet their major goals. Sometimes companies will offer up performance bonuses when they cannot give you a salary increase.

I am an over performer. I would often negotiate for a performance bonus for a goal that the company thought that they'd never hit, and viola, I'd prove them wrong and get the bonus nonetheless. Everyone was happy. It was a win /win.

Additional Vacation Days

Another good option \to consider is to ask for additional time off. Even a boss with limited power can often times grant you additional paid time off. Depending upon the phase of life that you are in, time off could be more valuable to you than money.

Flex Scheduling or Job Share

You could consider asking for and getting a flex schedule. I once proposed four, ten hours days and loved the schedule. I received three days off a week, and the team rotated days off. It was a fantastic schedule. (I'd take one of those now!) Another great option is to propose a job share where two people work one position, allowing you to work part time and be home while your kids are young as opposed to working a full-time schedule or not working at all.

Maybe there is a new role that you could propose, i.e. become the social media expert in your business that manages all social content and works entirely from home. Maybe you are interested in a national travel role, even though today the role doesn't exist. Consider creating the job of your dreams on paper and seeing if the company will consider putting you in it. You've got nothing to lose and everything to gain. When you risk nothing, you gain nothing. Decide to take a risk, make a recommendation, create a new idea, and see what happens. You'll be surprised at the result. They will say 'yes' to some of the things that you expect them to say 'no' to.

Work at Home

Propose an option to work at home full- or part-time. Consider starting with just one day a week. Most employees find that with the modernization of technology, they can be very efficient at home. You might discover that you get more done, are more focused, and perform better with an occasional work day at home. You get busy and you go from meeting to meeting without actually accomplishing anything. To make the most money, you must figure out what would make you the most productive, and then make it happen.

3 Days to a Raise

Companies Run on a Budget Just Like You Do

Companies have a set spending limit. They have a budget. That budget has to accomplish all the stated goals and achievements for that company. Similar to your own checkbook, they often run short on what they would really like to spend and accomplish. Therefore companies will take a minimalist approach. The minimum amount that they can pay you to keep you is the amount they will offer. They can only afford to pay raises to the top 10% in the company. When you demand a raise, a quick offer without debate or a discussion, could indicate that you are more underpaid than you originally thought. Normally, they tell you that they have nothing in the budget to give you. I have heard this over and over again, each time I received a substantial raise (after MUCH deliberation). So, needless to say, they really could give me a raise, but were just trying not to. If you are truly valuable, they can definitely find you additional pay.

My first experience with this was five years into one of my employments. Having stayed at a technology company longer than people generally stay, I was underpaid. Not only that, but my research showed that I had contributed significantly to the bottom line. One example was an email from a major customer that indicated that their several hundred million dollar deal would not have signed without my influence. I had many such examples that I had saved. My current boss had taken the credit for my success, and although my department was slated for bonuses, I hadn't received any.

My first step was doing the research. I had to determine if my belief that I was underpaid could be substantiated. I had to determine my worth outside of the company, to then be able to determine my worth within the company. I polished up my resume and began interviewing for positions at other companies. At the time, it was the only way I knew to discuss salaries and to determine my market worth. Today, with internet searching tools and salary surveys that you can purchase, there are many options. Not only did I discover that I was underpaid, but I received a job offer from the competition. It included a $5,000 sign on bonus, as well as a $15,000 annual bonus. The base salary was $15,000 more than I was currently making. It also included 1500 stock options per year. This brought my new offer to:

$15,000 increase in base pay
$15,000 annual bonus
$ 5,000 sign on bonus
_____
$35,000 more CASH in the first year   PLUS OPTIONS!

I had already had the discussion with my boss that I was not satisfied with my pay, and I had requested a pay raise, which was denied due to no money in the budget. I then sat down with my boss a second time. I said, " I love working here and have enjoyed the last five years at this company. Unfortunately, my salary has fallen significantly below market value, and I can't afford to stay here any longer. If you cannot help me get my salary in line with industry standards, I will be forced to leave. I have been offered higher pay at another company. "

Guess what? They were somehow able to find the money in their budget. I discovered one thing that day; if you are truly valuable and you have built your brand and are recognized for your contributions, your company may not want to let you go. Be prepared to go, though. You will only make more money if you are prepared to take the other offer, once you bring it up.

When was the last time you negotiated such a great deal for yourself, sufficient stock options, an incredible raise etc, as to enable you to retire young, or retire in the event of a buyout? You should be thinking that you can instead of thinking that it is impossible.

Rule #10: Don't Be Afraid to Talk Numbers with Your Network

You've been told not to tell anyone how much you make. The office politics have done an incredible job of teaching you to keep your mouth shut. All in all, it has simply enabled your employer to keep you in the dark on pay practices and comparable salaries. Thank goodness for the internet, salary surveys, and new web sites like glassdoor.com where you are finally able to start getting access to the numbers and see behind the curtain.

Don't be afraid to talk numbers with your network. It is always better to do this with a network that consists of people that don't work at the same company that you work at to avoid as many office politics as you can. Men do this and have an edge on us. You need to learn to be able to talk numbers. For those at other companies that you network with, talk numbers. Share salary information.

Talk about bonuses and stock options. You may feel more confident about asking for a raise if you find out that someone in the same position you have at another company is making 35% more. Numbers don't lie.

The company may not have the money to give you a raise, but you may find out that another company is paying twice what you are making for the same position. Knowledge is power and it is your obligation to get as much knowledge on this subject as humanly possible. After all, we are talking about your pay, your livelihood and your future.

Add New People to Your Network to Talk Money With

If you're thinking that there just isn't anyone in your network that you can talk numbers with, than remedy the situation. Add new people to your network that you can talk numbers with. Frankly, if you are in the majority of statistics for women, than you are good at relationship building, but don't take time out to network professionally. Once you do network, you are shy at asking them how much they make and what benefits, options and bonuses they've received. In general, men are better at these type of networking discussions. Many women are going it alone. You may be one of them that are trying to do it by yourself and it isn't paying off for you.

Sallie Krawcheck is an expert on networking. In a LinkedIn article she writes," You approach it (networking) half-heartedly because you sort of view networking as cheating. I honestly can't tell you how many women have told me this, particularly younger women. They feel like they should be able to make it "on their own merits" rather than also through whom they know. I wonder if this was the lesson we took away from those all of the fairy tales fed to us as little girls. Sleeping Beauty, Cinderella, Snow White....do the right thing, keep quiet and your prince will come, often aided by a fairy godmother. Newsflash: there are few HR fairy godmothers. Please network."

Networking gets a bad rap. People tell you to make hundreds of connections and create a vast network. I'm not advising that at all. I'm advising that you make one to three contacts with those you generally like and who work in similar roles within your industry. Form friendships and bonds and begin sharing details of salary information with them for the betterment of both of you.

I have taken this approach and some of them are now my closest friends. Don't think 'network' , think about creating lasting friendships with people in your industry that will last the test of time, give you insight into wage data, and provide you with a leg up for your next wage negotiation.

Find Salary Data Any Way You Can

Many industries publish salary surveys. Salary information can be viewed on salary.com or even purchased. Many resources for salary data is available via searches on the internet and through industry or trade groups. Generally these surveys are less than a hundred dollars and well worth the cost to find out what your market rate should be.

You can do a quick search on www.salary.com and find an idea of what differing titles pay. This is quick and easy. This is not nearly as complete as buying a full survey, but it can certainly give you an idea of where to start. Access www.salary.com and choose from a list of job titles that they have in their database. Within 10 seconds you can view the suggested salary. You owe it to yourself to click yourself into a more prepared idea of what you should be making.

Rule #11: See 'No' As a Speed Bump, Not a Stop Light

Most of the time when I tried to get a raise, I'd receive a big fat 'no'. I'd feel sympathy for my company and my boss and respond with, " I understand", or "It's okay" . I later found out my male counterparts were saying, "What the hell, seriously" After all the work I've done for the company this year and the amazing results I've accomplished." Whereas, I saw 'no' as a stop sign, they saw no as a speed bump. I would stop but they'd would only slow down and then drive right past me onward and upward to better positions and higher salaries, better college educations for their children and earlier retirements. Meanwhile, I only felt compassion and sympathy for a company that was not taking care of me and this weakness was putting my salary behind where it should be. Are you doing the same thing?

Don't make my mistake. This is a boxing match and the best action starts after round one. Round one is where the players are introduced, goals and objectives are identified and the crowd anxiously watches the match, sometimes picking a winner and a loser early on. The match is just beginning. Now is the time to kick it into high gear. It is time to double up production, work harder, and be more persuasive and persistent in the attempt to secure a raise. It is NOT the time to give up. It is not the right time to back down. Backing down easily is like giving your teenager the keys to the car and your debit card and saying, "See you in a few years." You're allowing your company to take advantage of you. You are allowing them to keep your wage lower than it should be. You are contributing to the national average of women being paid 30% below our male counterparts. Stop it now!

It doesn't make you rude or too aggressive to state your request and persistently pursue the right answer. It makes you a good businesswoman, one that understands how things work and is willing to fight for what's right. At your heart, you feel uncomfortable pressing for a raise. The same way that you were probably not the teenager trying to force your boyfriend to have sex with you with repeated requests and attempts, you are probably not pursuing a raise with persistent determination. You find it unappealing. You find it beneath you. You keep hoping you won't have to ask. Remember how many times he asked you? Some of you weren't even allowed to call a boy, he had to call you. He had to be the pursuer. He never gave up and neither do the men when it comes to pay raises. They are the squeaky wheels that are getting adequate compensation while we sit quietly by waiting for someone to recognize us and raise our pay.

You cannot give up. You cannot read this and then decide that well, you tried and failed. Persistence is the key.

Women have been sitting by for 50 years watching the men be more persistent than us and pushing past us on the wage index. It's time to stand up and not give up. Never passively decide that it cannot be better than it is today.

DAY 3: ASK: Prepare Your Exit Plan & Go Ask for the Raise

Start with an exit plan

No matter how ready you are to enact your plan, you will be more successful if you have prepared an exit plan. Sometimes, companies are not willing to pay you more. However, this doesn't mean that you are stranded or 'stuck' in your current position and wage. Sometimes, in order to achieve your full potential, you must explore other options. This will help you in a variety of ways. It will help you to understand what options are available to you and it will help you to confirm your market value. There is nothing more accurate than knowing what other positions are available and how much they pay.

On day 3 of your raise journey, you begin thinking about possible exit plans. You do not have to have an exit plan to ask for more money, but it is important to have thought through possible other companies and other positions that may be a perfect fit for you.

If you go to the well and are unsuccessful, then you will dive deeper into your exit plan options and capturing the action steps necessary to begin some occasional job searching.

You have to ask

The whole book has culminated in this one small section. Here we will explore exactly how to ask, the words to use, and the attitude that will accompany you in the door. There is no way around it. You have to ask. I recognize that you hate rejection. You would rather not ask and have to hear a no. I'm asking you to think about it like a business transaction. When you make a purchase, that purchase costs x dollars. You either decide to buy the item based on the stated value on the tag, or you pass. This concept applies to you at work. The company will either see your value as more than they currently pay you, and offer to pay you more, or they won't and they will leave you at your current pay leaving you to seek higher pay elsewhere.

Either way, you've will have asked. Either way, you didn't lose your current standing. The final, and most important phase in this journey is to ask and there is no time like the present. Email or call your superior to request a meeting. If you have a review coming up, that would be a good time to discuss your salary.

To make it easier, I'll model the way to ask. Verbal points to cover in your ask:

- Start by giving them some history of your experience and life at the company.
- Describe the benefits you've brought the company in performance, cost savings, production, customer satisfaction, ect.

- Be appreciative and thankful
- Explain why you are asking
  - Are you under market value?
  - Have you been offered another position paying more?
- Be specific in your ask
  - Ask for a dollar amount or a percentage

A sample request would sound something like this:

> "I've been at this company for X years. I've been able to grow in my career and learnings, and for that I'm very thankful. Can we work together to get me a raise, getting me closer to my market value?

> I have a dilemma. My salary has fallen below my market value. I am requesting that you raise my pay. I enjoy working here and want to build my career here.

> I've been able to bring in X dollars in the last year, and lead y projects to completion. Since the company has been able to achieve 123 in revenue, I'd like to request a raise of z dollars based on my performance.

> In order to bring my salary commensurate with the experience that I've achieved over the last several years at our company, I'd like to request a raise of XYZ dollars."

3 Days to a Raise

Creating the right mindset, not ruled by emotions

Start with these 5 actions to set yourself up for the most success.

- Make an appointment
- Show up on time
- Be prepared with data
- Ask for how much and why- be specific
- Then shhhhhh- be silent and wait for an answer

Understanding your boss, differing personalities and how to maneuver them

I wish I could say that a good strategy would work with all bosses, but it won't. There are multiple personalities that you run into. Let's review 3 personalities and how to approach each.

1) **Cheap Chip**
You may have the boss that is super cheap. This is a hard one to negotiate with. Tie your raise directly to achievements for the company. Often direct incentives based on performance work better than a raise to overall salary. He may never give you a raise and you may be forced to exercise an exit plan. More on that later.

2) **Too Busy to be bothered Bob**
It is hard to get his attention and keep it. He is always busy and it is hard to get his focused attention. For this personality type, I suggest having something in writing prepared. The combination of the written leave behind, and

the verbal request works the best. Follow up with them in 7 days, 14 days, and 21 days. Be persistent.

3) Avoiding Alex

Alex avoids conflict and often avoids discussions with you. Since you rarely talk to him, asking for a raise is difficult. Schedule a meeting with him. Make a strong case and hope like heck that he sees it your way. Give him a date that you will follow up and leave the meeting without conflict.

Don't back down, and prepare your exit plan

If you truly know that you are under market value and they say 'no', ask for a future date for consideration. You deserve it, they are counting on the fact that you will just go away and never bring it up again. Don't go away. Start applying for other positions if your company doesn't respond. Find a better paying job. Start by preparing for the exit plan:

1) Update your resume
2) Make your LinkedIN sizzle- many recruiters and employers search for candidates on LinkedIn
3) Call a recruiter, they will help you with great (free) advice
4) Click 'APPLY' on 2 websites and fill out the forms for a job you'd love to have

Keep performing, know your strengths, and stand out

Often when you ask for a raise and don't get it, you stop performing. You stop giving it your all. YOU MUST keep

3 Days to a Raise

performing EVEN if you feel like you are underpaid. It is imperative that you continue to blow out the seams of your job no matter what happens in steps 1-9. YOU are a brand. YOU need to rock it. Do a fabulous job and higher pay will follow. I'm counting on your success. Good luck.

Drive toward the goal- Go Make it Happen

I've worked hard. I have received more job offers than I could ever take. I've been given more options at companies than they've granted any other employee at the company. But, I don't want to stop with benefiting only myself and my family. **I want women to learn from my struggles and my achievements**. I want your life to be better forever. You can impact your future. Don't walk away from this book without an action plan. Don't continue to accept the status quo. Do not comfortably sit back and accept #2 positions when you should be #1.

I'm breaking all the rules to give you this advice, and risking my own security and livelihood. Please use this information to better your future and the future of all those coming behind you. I believe in you. Go make it happen!

Bethany A Williams

It's Time to ACT

Next Steps:

I have created a "3 Days to a Raise" video series to teach you EXACTLY how to do this by showing YOU what is holding you back—as well as detailed instructions on getting those high-level positions and pay increases.

This 3-part training seminar will help you increase your pay. It is for employees and entrepreneurs alike, helping you to negotiate for higher incomes and more business. This approach has helped numerous women raise their pay immediately, with opportunities to double your income. This video series can be found on my website: www.bethanyawilliams.com

For reading this book, I'll offer it to you free. Simply email me at the website and reference the book you've read and you'd like to watch the video for free. I'll respond with a code to get you on your journey.

Continue the journey. Invest in yourself. I'll teach you the words to say and how to do it. You deserve to make more and arrive in better positions:
http://bethanyawilliams.com/shop/

3 Days to a Raise

YOU Deserve A Raise!

Raise the Stakes, &
Raise your Pay

Bethany's Latest Video Seminar

References:

1) Why Men Need Women from the Sunday Review of the New York Times
http://www.nytimes.com/2013/07/21/opinion/sunday/why-men-need-women.html?pagewanted=all&_r=0
Adam Grant, author, July 20, 2013

2) Dell Lawsuit:
http://www.bloomberg.com/apps/news?pid=newsarchive&sid=aZtD.RbF.pjY
http://www.bizjournals.com/austin/print-edition/2011/01/14/dell-named-defendant-in-another.html?page=all
http://www.abajournal.com/news/article/dell_sued_over_claimed_concrete_ceiling/

3 Days to a Raise

Appendix: Not-for-Profit Company Research Guide

If you work for a non-profit, then there is a way to access and review financial information that they must file with the IRS. Some of you may be aware of this, but for those of you that are not, I'd like to introduce you to the IRS Form 990.

The IRS Form 990 is an annual reporting return that certain federally tax-exempt organizations must file with the IRS. It provides information on the filing organization's mission, programs, and finances. Most particularly to our discussion, it lists salaries for Director level employees and above. It is a good barometer to start your research in order to compare your salary with those of others at comparable organizations or to seek out information on positions that you are aspiring to obtain. I once worked for a promotion towards a position for 10 years while working at Sharp Healthcare in San Diego, all the while completely unaware of that position would pay if I indeed was promoted into it. It seems so silly in retrospect, but what are you working towards? Do you know what the position pays that you are seeking? If you don't, it is time to do some research.

The organizations that have to file Form 990s are as follows:

- o   Most federally tax-exempt organizations, with the exception of churches and state institutions.

- o   All 501(c)(3) private foundations, regardless of income

If the organization that you work for is a non-profit, then they have been filing this form with the IRS and it is discoverable.

For those of you not familiar with this filing requirement, you are probably thinking, that's nice, but how would I get my hand on those forms? These Form 990s are available for purchase on the website www.guidestar.org. Easy search features allow you to easily find the organization that you are interested in and view the report.

As an example, from www.guidestar.org , search for UT Southwestern in the search bar, and a listing will display with all selections with those words in the title.

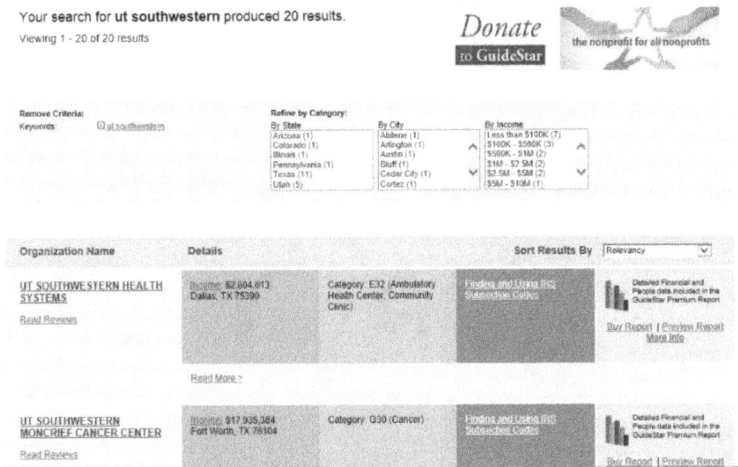

You can choose to further delineate the listing by filtering by state, city, or income of the organization. In the far right column, you can choose to purchase the report. Reports can be purchased for $125 a report (at present time of publication) or you can secure monthly access for $250 a month.

3 Days to a Raise

Detailed information on reading the form 990 can be found at: http://www.npccny.org/Form_990/990.htm .

Appendix: For-Profit Company Research Guide

For-profit companies can also be researched by pulling the 10Ks. A Form **10-K** is an annual report required by the U.S. Securities and Exchange Commission (SEC), that gives a comprehensive summary of a company's financial performance. Since all companies are required to file these statements, it can help you find important information to help you on your salary journey. They include key information that will help you assess earning potential. The 10K will list the salaries for the key executives at the company. Find these forms easily by reviewing the SEC website information listed at
http://www.sec.gov/edgar.shtml#.VFUVeYm9LCQ .

Here is a link to the 10K Wikipedia definition:
http://en.wikipedia.org/wiki/Form_10-K . Spend time familiarizing yourself with this form and understanding how to easily pull it online and learn from its many treasures. It will be worth the time you spend researching.

3 Days to a Raise

Connect with the Author via

Facebook

Scan

Twitter

Website: http://www.BethanyAWilliams.com

Twitter: BethanyaWill
Facebook: WinLifeStrategy
YouTube: BethanyAWilliams

Bethany A. Williams

See Bethany's other Winning Strategies series books:

Winning Strategies for Women:

This book provides practical, step-by-step advice for excelling in business, strategies for keeping your job, getting promotions and pay raises, and receiving more recognition in the process.

Learn how to create a situation where YOU become the one working for the greatest companies, achieving the best assignments and receiving the highest pay!

Order it online: http://goo.gl/2f6Xpr

From Mother to Mentor & Father to Coach:

Are fights erupting in your household? Do you have a teenager with raging hormones? This practical guide book will rescue you from the dilemmas that you face with your teenager.

Brimming with tips and insights, it will assist you moving out of the combat zone. Your role as parent officially changes to helpful mentor and coach.

Order it online:  http://goo.gl/QBtk1n

Brand YOU:

Create a Personal Brand for YOU that sells your skills to a market wrought with competition and an ever-decreasing number of available jobs.

In the pages of this book, you will get a boost at creating your own personal brand. You will be inspired and motivated with suggestions and ideas. This book will give what you need to create a list of 'To Dos' to walk you toward increased profitability and success.
Order it online: http://goo.gl/eZ3KFV

3 Days to a Raise

Live Your Dreams:

Are you living your dreams? Can you accept that you can create a new reality? Make a plan and make it happen. What are you waiting for? Get off the couch of your life and start living the life you were born to live today.

This book was written to motivate you toward living your dream life. It is intended to guide you to the life that you yearn for. It will motivate you into a new day and a new life. It will catapult you into your dream world. Start making a new plan today!

Order it online: http://goo.gl/HjJ9wu

CEO of YOU:

This is do-it-yourself career management at its best. You are CEO of your career and your destiny. Learn to manage your career and earnings for guaranteed success.

This book will guide you through the steps necessary to take your career and earnings to the next level.

• Build a personal board of directors for you
• Market yourself in a new way
• Learn and incorporate necessary skills that you will need for the next 10 years

Order it online: http://goo.gl/s207Ge

Bethany A. Williams

3 Days to a Raise VIDEO SERIES

Video 1: We look at the numbers and review what you should be making and how to find the information & commonly held faulty belief systems that you are holding onto that are keeping you from making the pay that you deserve.

Video 2: We address some big items in #2: "The 11 New Rules for Getting Paid." There are new rules for getting paid. In order to make money in this new economy, you must understand the 11 new rules for getting paid.

Review stock options and stock grants, find out common compensation practices and learn the secrets to compensation.

Video 3: This is titled, "Preparing your exit plan, and THE ASK." This section drills down into the details of the exit plan and how to add leverage to your situation.

We will model the 'ASK' and walk you through the words to use. I'll tell you exactly what to say, and how to go get that raise.

3 Days to a Raise

3 Days to a Raise:

This video series can be found on my website:

www.bethanyawilliams.com

Best Wishes for MUCH Success,

Bethany A Williams